Bed Bugs

Learn How to Kill Bed Bugs and Prevent Bed Bug Bites

(How to Get Rid of Bed Bugs without Toxic Chemicals or Insecticides)

Aaron Dyer

Published By **Darby Connor**

Aaron Dyer

Bed Bugs: Learn How to Kill Bed Bugs and Prevent Bed Bug Bites (How to Get Rid of Bed Bugs without Toxic Chemicals or Insecticides)

ISBN 978-1-7775976-8-9

Legal & Disclaimer

The information contained in this book is not designed to replace or take the place of any form of medicine or professional medical advice. The information in this book has been provided for educational & entertainment purposes only.

The information contained in this book has been compiled from sources deemed reliable, and it is accurate to the best of the Author's knowledge; however, the Author cannot guarantee its accuracy and validity and cannot be held liable for any errors or omissions. Changes are periodically made to this book. You must consult your doctor or get professional medical advice before using any of the suggested remedies, techniques, or information in this book.

Upon using the information contained in this book, you agree to hold harmless the Author from and against any damages, costs, and expenses, including any legal fees potentially resulting from the application of any of the information provided by this guide. This disclaimer applies to any damages or injury caused by the use and application, whether directly or indirectly, of any advice or information presented, whether for breach of contract, tort, negligence, personal injury, criminal intent, or under any other cause of action.

You agree to accept all risks of using the information presented inside this book. You need to consult a professional medical practitioner in order to ensure you are both able and healthy enough to participate in this program.

Table Of Contents

Chapter 1: The Bed Bug Problem

The bed bugs will not bite you unless they get your shoe.

This bed bug problem will only get worse. Not only do you need to learn why it is worsening, but how to effectively and safely handle the situation.

It is not the lexicologists who put spaces between bed and bug, but the entomologists who do research on bed bugs. This book can help to create some space between you. The bed bug is also called chinches or chintzes. It can be classified as house bugs, wall louse and red coats.

DESCRIPTION AND HABITS OF YOUR ENEMY

Bed bugs are flattened, small brownish insects that look like an apple seed. They feed exclusively on mammals and birds. Even though the bed bug is more likely to prefer humans (Cimex. lectularius), it can also feed on other warm-blooded species, including dogs, cats, bats and birds. They are approximately 3/16" in length and reddishbrown with flattened, oval-shaped bodies. They may be confused with fleas (or ticks), cockroaches (or carpet beetles), cockroaches (or other household bugs), or cockroaches.

They are roughly the same size as Lincoln on a pennies. On their legs, bed bug adults are covered with many setae. They can attach themselves to flannel bedding or even the hooked hairs at the top of fresh leaves of garden beans. In the presence of blood, bedbugs swell up and change their color from brown to dark. In general, bed bugs have a lifespan of one to two years.

NYMPHS

Immature bedbugs (nymphs), which are much smaller than adults and of a lighter colour, look similar but have less size. Bed bugs are not able to fly or leap, but instead they crawl over walls, floors and ceilings. The bed bugs' eggs are very small, about the size of dust particles. They can be difficult to see even with magnification. Bed bug females lay eggs in small cracks near their host. She firmly cements the eggs in place. With frequent feedings, such as twice weekly, and at temperatures of 77°F, a female will lay approximately 345 egg. They have been compared to the rubber fillers of fountain-pen refills. This cap is "like an manhole cover" and it falls off as soon as the eggs hatch. Unhatched egg are transparent, and have a pearly color. However, hatched eggs will be translucent. Incubation time varies depending on the temperature. These newly-emerged nymphs look straw-colored, and they are about the size of a pinhead.

FEMALES

If they cannot get any more blood, females quit laying at 11 days. You can protect your home by moving the bed further away from the walls. Any surface can be made too slippery for them by applying a thin layer of Talc. Use talc tapes, silicone or double-sided tapes, with sticky sides up. (Or petroleum jelly brushed on the ground) You can also protect the edges of your bed by using duct or talc tapes.

In order to mature, bed bugs shed their skin five times. You must give them a fresh blood meal between each successive moult. The bed bugs will mature completely in one month under ideal conditions. A cooler temperature or a limited supply of blood will slow their process.

Bed bugs have a high level of adaptability and resilience. Both nymphs and adult bed bugs can go for long periods of time without feeding. It is mainly human blood that they feed on, however, they will also suck up blood from birds, bats, other animals. This could lead to them being a vector of diseases from whatever they ate before!

Between meals, bedbugs do not clean themselves or brush their hair! They can wait up to 6 months before they feed!

It is true that bedbugs can survive without food for 18 months, and up to 1 year. At cooler temperatures, their ability to survive for longer periods without feeding on blood is increased. In temperature--controlled buildings, a more typical duration is about 2 to 6 months. In order to'starve an infestation out,' it is often not feasible to leave buildings unoccupied. If vacated apartments infested with bedbugs spread out to adjacent units or just reduce activity.

Before World War II bed bug infestations in the United States were quite common. In the United States, bed bugs almost disappeared during the 1950s with DDT sprays on baseboards. In the USA, bedbugs have been attacking USA residents with a new vengeance since 2003. And this epidemic has no signs of slowing. 93% are currently at risk.

Since the beginning of the decade, both entomologists, and professionals in pest control, have been reporting an increase in bed bug outbreaks all over the U.S. (in cities from New York, to Honolulu) especially in hospitals, hotels, apartment buildings, clinics, theaters, washrooms, office building, schools, refuges, transportation, college dorms (all places that are warm and with high turnover), and no one (except the author) can explain why.

It is my belief that the primary reason behind the explosive growth of these unwanted "guests" in recent years has been the fact that all currently approved pesticides are no longer effective against bed bugs! It is for this reason most pest management companies do not use toxic chemicals exclusively in order to fight bed bug invasions. The "modern' pesticides and insects are useless now against bed bugs.

In addition, bedbugs are prolific breeding and predators. Bed bugs are also known to feed on other warm-bodied species, like bats. These bugs can be found in shelters, such as those along trails or cabins located at parks and summer camps. In many cases, bed bugs that infest urban homes are spread by remote camping grounds. Laura Kruger of California Department of Health pointed out that at 70 degrees F., 40 bedbugs placed in one room would multiply to 5905 in six months. What does it mean? They multiply incredibly fast. You can see that the bed bug epidemic is a result of both a lack an effective pesticide, and an incredible cycle for reproduction.

Chapter 2: Non-Natural Methods For Killing Bed Bug

It is important to note that bed bugs can be sensitive to both changes in temperature and heat at any stage of their life cycle. It is estimated that the thermal death temperature for bed bugs ranges from 111°F to 113°F. Increasing the room's temperature up to 97°F to 99°F will also help to kill large numbers of them. It is possible to eliminate bed bug infestations by increasing the room temperature from 97 degrees F. to 99 degrees F.

For localized bed bug infestations you can use either a heat source like a blow dryer, or steam from a cleaner. It is possible to kill bedbugs by using a fine dust. This will block their breathing holes, located on the side of each insect. Add a small amount of dust (talcum, Diatomaceous or other fine powders) to your dry vacuum cleaner or to soapy water when you rinse your vac. This will kill the bed bugs that you pick up.

Even bed bugs' eggs are killed at low temperatures (30 degrees F. - 48 degrees F.). Adults, nymphs, and even their eggs can die from these temperatures in just 30 to 50 day. Close off the bedroom infested with bed bugs and leave it unheated throughout the Winter. Although it may not be an easy solution to solve, it is a good way to eradicate localized infestations. A carbon dioxide fogging of the area and mattress will quickly kill bedbugs.

The bed bug life cycle can last up to 5 days in temperatures as low as 14 degrees F. You can either place your mattress and springs in the sauna, or put them in a "bag" of black heavy visquine that is duct-taped together. Or, you can use dry ice (1#-3#) in a small paper bag and add it directly on top (of the plastic covered mattress). The bed bug colonies can only be eradicated by thorough and regular cleaning.

To dust into the cracks in floors and baseboards you can use talcum, medicated bath or body powders, food-grade diatomaceous soil (DE) and even Comet. Safe Solutions Tweetmint Enzyme and/or other borax products can be used as required to thoroughly vacuum and clean.

INSPECTION & MONITORING

Diatomaceous Earth can be used to kill bed bugs, as well as a blowdryer and any other method mentioned. After you learn these tricks, killing bedbugs is not a problem. Real problem: kill ALL them to prevent their return. That requires a complete and intelligent examination.

After you have used one of the strategies listed above to control bed bugs, monitor the affected area. The infested areas can be inspected at night using a bright red lamp and magnifying glass (bed bugs do not see the red light, so they will try to avoid it). Seal cracks or crevices with spray foam. Caulk them and paint the area.

Not to mention, spiders as well as American roaches and Pharaoh ants have been observed eating bedbugs.

An inspection will be your most effective bed bug treatment. An inspection will help you eliminate all of the bed bugs. It is impossible to eliminate bed bugs without finding them. You will see them reproduce, and an infestation will occur again. Examine your bed and linens carefully. After feeding, bed bugs will migrate from the beds to closets, dressers and cracks in the walls. It can be difficult to find your hidden enemy. He often suggests inspecting by night only using a magnifying light and bright red lights.

Check the smell of the place. Infected bedbugs might expel an odor that smells similar to raspberries. But this smell is rarely noticeable except when there are severe infestations. So it's not recommended that you rely solely on smell, particularly during a first inspection. Inspect the bedding, couch, chair, camping, and sleeping gear, as well as all furniture. You can also inspect suitcases (gently), outlets, picture frames or clothing. You should carefully inspect the carpet tack strip and any loose wallpaper.

Examine all rooms, apartments vacant, summer camps and outdoor sheds for animals, barns or coops. Check all areas that are secluded, hot, dark and in close proximity to people or pets. With a hand-magnifying lens and bright light, you can better see bed bugs. You should inspect your home at the appropriate times. Bed bugs normally feed during the night. However, you can find them hiding at other times of the day, in small crevices on your mattress or in any tight space.

Bed bugs are small and light brown. Bed bug nymphs have a smaller size and a lighter colour. Check for the eggs and skins of bedbugs. They are tiny, white and hard to notice. Light brown encasements can be seen on skin sheds or molting. If you notice small dark dots, this could be bed bug waste. It is important to thoroughly inspect, vacuum and treat each room in your apartment or home.

You should spend your efforts inspecting the areas where you find them most often. It is because bed bug bodies are so adapted that they can fit and hide easily in small cracks and crevices. Bed bugs tend to be nocturnal and active at night. However, during the daylight hours they will hide near to their previous feeding site.

All bedbugs will initially be located in or around sleeping areas. This includes futons (couch), beds, and couches. Bed bugs are able to live in virtually any crevice. Mattresses and box springs are difficult to successfully treat. They may either need to simply be discarded, or they can be covered with a protective covering. Infestations of bedbugs tend to spread outside the sleeping area, which makes inspections more challenging. If you have a bed bug infestation, the sooner you deal with it, the better.

Remove all drawers on nightstands. Desks and Dressers. Flip the entire piece of furniture to clean and inspect all bed bugs' hiding places. Check all folds, crevices, and seams on headboards, mattresses, boxes springs, and bed frames. It is important to disassemble the bed in order to inspect all seams, surfaces and folds. Box springs are a great place for bed bugs, as they can be hidden along seams or underneath the mattress, at the point where it rests. You can remove the dust cover if it is there to inspect and possibly treat bed bugs. The bed bug prefers to stay on fabric and wood more than glass, metal or plastic. The wooden support boards, if they are present, need to be taken out and examined closely, since bedbugs tend to gather where these ends rest against the bed frame. It is important to remove and examine headboards that have been attached to walls.

Look behind the head board when renting your hotel room. In addition, bedbugs can be found in the items kept under beds. The seams along with the skirts or folds in fabric of upholstered sofas, recliners, and chairs should be carefully examined. The bed bugs are often found in recliners, sofas and futons. As with beds, these items can be tricky to deal with and need to sometimes be disposed.

Bed bugs usually hide in large groups. Their excrement can leave dark spots on these hiding places. The communal hideouts will contain un--hatched, newly-hatched, or scabby brown nymphs as well as clusters with various bed bugs.

The rusty reddish marks on mattresses or bedsheets that appear when someone rolls over in the middle of the night to crush a bedbug can indicate an infestation. In the event that bed bug infestations persist, bed bugs are likely to spread throughout the entire building. It is then even more difficult to remove them. Bed bug infestations are more common if you travel, have bought or received used bedding, clothing, dishware, and furnishings. Bed bugs can be found if, when you wake up in the morning, you find yourself with itchy red bumps. It is important to note that bed bug bites do not always cause such reactions. To confirm, it is necessary to find and identify bed bugs, shed-skin, fecal marks, etc. All of this requires an expert's help.

BED BUG BITES AND HEALTH WORRIES

Bed bug saliva and bites can produce red itchy spots on your skin, usually on your neck, your face or your arms. Skin doctors often confuse bed bug bites with fleas, mosquitoes, or even scabies. Make sure you are certain that they are actually from bedbugs. Bed bug bites are usually found on sleeping pets or people. When they can't feed on people or pets at night they feed them during the day, especially if it is when they normally sleep or rest. The bed bug bite is not painful, so many victims don't even know they were bitten. The bed bug attaches itself with its claws. Next, it inserts a beak that has two stylets. Nymphs feed up to 3 minutes. Adults may continue to sucke your blood as long as 10-15 minutes.

Some people will experience itching, swelling, and even burning when bitten by bed bugs, based on their susceptibility. Others may not react at all. In those who do experience irritation, it is usually due to the venom the bug injects as it feeds. The bump may appear as an itchy, raised wheal, and may contain 2 to 3 closely spaced punctures. Bed bugs don't normally live for long on the body or head like lice, crabs, and other parasites. Bed bugs that have eaten their food will slowly move to a hidden location in order to digest it.

Chapter 3: The Bed Bug-Borne Diseases

Historically, it was believed that bed bugs couldn't transmit disease. Today, we are aware that bedbugs can carry dangerous pathogens. Inflammation and itching caused by bed bug stings require some medical attention. It is possible to prescribe antihistamines, corticosteroids or antibiotic ointments in order to decrease allergic reactions. In addition to reducing your quality of life, bed bugs can also have an emotional impact. This can be due to discomfort, allergens, sleeplessness and anxiety. It is possible that some "friends" will leave when they learn you have these pests. From the very beginning, man has shared a home with bed bugs and they have fed on them. By biting, bedbugs are known to infect people with disease and spread it. This can cause allergic and digestive reactions and nerve and stomach disorders. The bed bug has been proven to transmit the anthrax-causing agents, plague-causing agents, typhus and tularemia-causing agents in lab tests. If children are living in heavily infested households, they become pale and listless. From glands found on the thorax, bed bugs emit an odor. Some have described the smell as sickeningly sweetness, musty and/or crushed raspberries or soda pop syrup.

You need to know that bed bugs are capable of transmitting diseases. If you hear someone say otherwise, they are not experts on bed bugs.

Researchers in Vancouver recently reported that they had found bed bugs with methicillin--resistant Staphylococcus aureus, or MRSA. The researchers crushed and analysed five bed bugs, and three of them contained MRSA. MRSA is a superbacterium resistant to the most common antibiotics. The two other samples had vancomycin--resistant Enterococcus faecium, or VRE, a less dangerous antibiotic--resistant bacteria. Mayo Clinic states that the bugs could carry bacteria that can cause hepatitis and

Chagas. Recent studies showed that bed bugs are capable of transferring dangerous bacteria to human hosts. It is especially dangerous for women aged over 55 because their susceptibility increases to all the diseases carried by these small blood sucking vampiric insects.

BED BUGS - How to get rid of them

Contrary to the Author's recommendation, many recommend the use dozens fragrant dryer sheets and/or insect repellents as well lights in order to repel bedbugs. Dryer sheets, according to the Author, are dangerous. Here is a list of just some of the chemicals found in fabric softeners and and even in formaldehyde--free dryer sheets from this website and their health effects: http://www.ghchealth.com/forum/post--325.html

Benzyl acetate linked to pancreatic tumors

Benzyl Alcohol: Upper respiratory tract irritant

The Environmental Protection Agency has listed ethanol as a Hazardous Waste and it can lead to central nervous disorders.

This synthetic form of limonene has been linked to cancer.

A--Terpineol Can Cause Respiratory Problems, Central Nervous System Damage, Death and Fatal Edema

Ethyl Acetate - a narcotic in the EPA Hazardous Waste list

Camphor causes central nervous system disorders

Chloroform, a carcinogen and neurotoxic substance

Linalool causes Central Nervous System Disorders

The chemical pentane can be dangerous if breathed in!

It appears that conventional insecticides (DEET), commonly used against ticks, mosquitoes and bed bugs do not work nearly as effectively. In order to prevent bed bug bites, it is not recommended that you apply conventional insect repellents just before going to sleep. The lights will not deter the bed bug population, which is hungry and adapts their feeding pattern to that of the host.

What caused this terrible infestation?

Bed bugs: Where do they come from?

The bed bugs will easily enter your building via luggage, clothes, suitcases, bedding, office furniture, purses or backpacks. The likelihood of bed bugs infecting warm hotel rooms, medical facilities, office buildings, schools and other apartments is higher. Small and agile, bed bugs can crawl through suitcases and backpacks to reach your belongings. If you are bringing secondhand couches, tables, chairs, cushions, sheets, picture frames and desks into your warm house, they will be attracted to them. Bed bugs may also hitchhike on clothing, shoes, or even wheelchairs. As soon as bed bugs enter a home, they disperse quickly. They can even crawl from floor-to-floor. In his youth, the author recalls people not letting him place their coats or jackets on top of his Parents bed during a visit out of fear it might be infested.

You can also eliminate or reduce bedbug infestations by cleaning regularly and properly.

DO THEY REALLY ACT LIKE BED BUGS?

The world is home to at least 92 bed bug species and relatives. This includes the tropical Cimexhemipterus bed bug, as well as the swallow bug, Oeciaus Vicaruis, and swift bug, Cimexopsis Nycatalis. They are all capable of feeding occasionally on humans, animals, birds, and bats.

Cimex pilosellus, (Horv.), and Cimex adhuctus, (Barber), are the two "bed" bug species that you will find in bat colonies. Cimex Adjuctus Barber and Cimex Pilosellus Horv. Bird and bat bugs look very much like the common bedbug, although they are not as aggressive in their infestation of structures. Bird bugs, bat bugs or both can move when their primary hosts are gone. They may also wander if rodents and construction have been done to exclude them. The "regular' bed bugs are very similar, and they will not bother you. However, other bed bug species can also be found that are parasites on other hosts, such as bats, swallows chimney swifts pigeons etc.

When you see a bat bug, which is usually found in the rooms below the attic or if you notice a bird fly by your windows and it bites you or someone in your family, locate the entire nesting site. Vacuum thoroughly once the debris from the room has been cleared. Wear a mask and protective clothes. Safe Solutions, Inc. is used to clean, spray, or power wash an area thoroughly. Then, use an enzyme cleaner containing peppermint oil and/or Borax or sodium borate. Dust the area thoroughly with Food grade Diatomaceous. When bat or bird insects are in the house, you should first focus on the roosting/nesting locations. Remove all birds, pets, and nests from the home. The areas around these areas should be properly treated before the other blood eaters start to look towards you.

Bed bugs can be prevented from entering your home by following these steps:

Bed bugs should be checked on all furniture that has been used, rented, or purchased.

Caulk is a great way to prevent bed bugs from entering your home. It doesn't matter if bed bugs aren't present yet. Caulk will stop them and other pests entering your home.

Never put suitcases or bags on beds, floors or the floor while traveling. If you suspect bedbugs, use a surface like a solid table.

Inspect and clean thoroughly your entire home.

BED BUG INTERESTATIONS: How to Control Them

You can see that it can be challenging to identify and completely eliminate bed bug infestations. They can hide anywhere, so you need to be thorough with your vacuuming and treatment. Hire a professional to help you with pest control. A professional pest control expert will have the knowledge to know exactly where bed bugs are hiding and may even use dogs or monitors.

You still have to do something for them. Unlock all rooms and remove all extra clutter. Even a professional will find it hard to do a thorough treatment and inspection of the building because clutter is a great place for bed bugs. As bedbugs can eventually be found in your whole building, you should inspect it all.

If I repeat myself again, the best place to look for bed bugs is in the bedroom or wherever people sleep. This is why these bugs are known as "bedbugs". So start there, then carefully inspect seams, folds, crevices, bed frames, and headboards. You may not find bed bugs around the beds. However, there could be other hiding places. You should always spend the majority of time in your bedroom inspecting, cleaning, and treating bed bugs, especially at the beginning stages. In larger bed bug infestations, bed bugs will spread to nearby places. This makes it difficult to treat.

This is why I repeat this info so often: if you do not find the hiding places of bed bugs you cannot achieve 100% extermination! Bed bug infestations can keep on recurring if you don't know where they are hiding. If you don't do a thorough inspection, I would rather that you read the instructions again than to have several bed bug infestations.

Examine cracks, crevices or bed frames regularly. This is particularly important if your bed frame is made of wooden. Monitoring with traps and interception tapes. If you are vacuuming, you should add soapy or talcum dust to the rinse and vacuum (or talcum to a dry vacuum) in order to eliminate any bed bugs that you may have picked up.

HABITAT ALTERATION

Altering Habitats or eliminating conditions that promote infestation is the first, and most effective control. It is vital to exclude these other creatures, as bedbugs can also feed on rodents. Vermin proofing all the infested structures can be a difficult task. Remove rodents, birds, bats and squirrels. Caulk all cracks, crevices, and joints. Vacuum mattresses, walls, floors, carpet, drapes, etc. Cleaning is important, particularly with diluted peppermint enzyme cleaners. Replace all bedding daily, or at least once a week. Use borax to wash the sheets (120° F minimum). DE of food-grade is ideal for dusting lightly on infestations. As bed bugs only crawl, move your bed away from a wall. Use duct or DE tape with the sticky side facing up or silicone or double-sided tape to further protect against bed bug attacks.

INSIDE:

Get rid of all the clutter, and then use a Dehumidifier.

By vacuuming all the hiding spots, bed bugs and their eggs are removed.

Launder all beddings in borax at least every week. Dust the cracks in drawers, electrical outlets and all other surfaces with Talcum.

Use diluted Safe Solutions, Inc.

You can also screen and caulk the entrances. Dust lightly with Comet® or Food-grade FD.

Protect mattresses by storing them in an area that is well-ventilated. Caulk every crack and crevice. Reglue the wallpaper.

Do not place mattresses in cots if they're not going to be used. This will prevent the nesting of mice. Prior to using your mattresses, fumigate them with carbon dioxide.

You can seal off any holes or openings by caulking and sealing them completely.

In the last resort, you can use Food-grade Diatomaceous (DE) or silica Aero Gel Dust.

Opening and vacuuming cabinets and drawers. It will discourage rodents and their nests.

Make crawl spaces visible and accessible by light and air flow, but not to rodents.

Regularly clean using diluted peppermint-borax enzyme cleaners.

OUTSIDE:

Removing all the wood and other debris away from the house.

Remove all vegetation, including weeds & shrubs from around the foundation.

Take out all the garbage, and eliminate rodents.

BED BUG TREATMENT # 1. Vacuuming and Steam Cleaning

You should vacuum and steam clean your entire room, especially the mattress and pillow infested areas. To add to the control, wash/clean with 1/2 cup of Borax or diluted peppermint enzyme cleaners per gallon. To begin with, it is best to take apart the bed. Then clean everything inside the room with Borax and diluted peppermint cleaners. Use diluted peppermint borax enzyme cleaners to steam or vacuum clean the entire room.

Caulk, seal and caulk again each room. It is not acceptable to have bed bugs on your body! The rodents that are inside should be caught and removed. Next, mop the floor and wash it with enzyme cleaners mixed with either peppermint DE or food grade de and/or/or/or/or/or/or/or/or/or/or/or/or/or/or/or/and/or/or/or/or/or/or/or/or/or/or/or/or/or/or/
and/or/or/or/or/or/or/or/or/or/or/or/or/or/or diluted with Desiccating dusts may be applied to cracks and crevices, if required. You can spray or clean with an enzyme cleaner that contains peppermint oil and borax. Be sure to caulk/seal every opening, and fix any loose wallpaper. Use of ultrasonic repellents is not effective. Avoid using space treatments of poisonous pesticides. These are dangerous and ineffective for bedbugs. You should read, understand and comply with all labels.

Chapter 4: High Temperatures

Heat can kill all stages of bed bugs – eggs, larvae pupae, adults. The optimal temperature for all insects is the one that allows them to thrive, reproduce and survive. A lethal range of temperatures is also set for all insects, where they will die at any stage in their lifecycle. All bed bug populations can be eradicated safely and efficiently by setting temperatures at the lethal level. Steam or even extremely hot water (120+ F..), will kill bedbugs. If you live in a tropical country, it is possible to soak your bed in hot water for a few hours and place the mattress out in sunlight. As the sun dries your mattress, the hot water alone will eliminate all the bed bugs.

TIME

In order to effectively treat bed bug infestations, the treatment time will be a major factor. Treatment time is dependent on many variables, such as humidity and clutter. It also depends on the structure of the room and the location. Using fans and heaters, you will need to warm each room from 140 degrees F up until 160. You should not heat your house above this temperature as it may result in a fire. This heat level will destroy the entire bed bug lifecycle, from eggs to adult bugs. Holding temperatures at this level for four hours is also enough time to kill common mold, allergens causing asthma and many other odors. Heat kills through dehydration or by drying out the insects. A high-heat/low-humidity atmosphere can cause insects to die because of lack moisture. The faster bedbugs die, the lower humidity in the heated room.

Treatment of localized bed bug invasions can be done by yourself with Hot Water or Dry Heat. It is a powerful contact killer and will eliminate bed bugs, as well their eggs.

The best way to rid your home of bed bugs is by using borax and hot water. In order to eliminate bed bugs, you should wash your bedding and linens in hot water and use borax. Dry them for several hours on high temperature. To be certain that your bed bug infestation is completely eradicated, repeat the cycle of drying several times. The hair dryer can be a useful tool in the fight against bed bugs. This is especially true if you know where to look for them. A hair dryer set to high temperature should be used for at least thirty seconds in cracks and crevices. This constant, dry heat blast will eliminate bedbugs immediately. It is important to use dry steam. While all methods of steaming increase the chance of mold in the home growing, steamers that are labeled "dry steam" reduce this risk significantly. You should not steam outlets. The combination of steam and electrical outlets is not good. It is vital to maintain the right temperature. Steam that is 120 degrees F should hit bedbugs. When purchasing a new steamer the manufacturer will list the maximum temperature for the tip. It is important that the surface registers a temperature at least 70 to 80 C immediately after treatment. Keep in mind that steam, which is hotter than air and may cause burns or even damage to some materials can harm you. Keep your focus and safety in mind.

Heat is a factor that bed bugs react to at all stages in their life cycle. It is important to note that the thermal death point of the bedbug common to most peoples is 111 to 113 degree F. However, even temperatures lower than this will be sufficient to kill a large number of bugs. It is possible to eliminate many infestations by increasing the temperature for an entire hour at 140 degrees F., or for several hours at 120 degrees F. If you want to kill bed bugs, use the steam cleaner or hair dryer weekly to steam in cracks or crevices. The same can be done by closing a room infested with bed bugs and not heating it in the cold. Also, carbon dioxide fumigation will work on both mattress and areas. If you want to kill bedbugs in their early stages, it is best to place your mattresses, springs, bedding and frames into a heavy plastic bag made out of visquine. This can be placed in the sunlight or a sauna. Cleaning thoroughly or using a vacuum cleaner will reduce the number of pests, but it will not be able to eliminate them completely. Last resort: Dust Food-grade Diatomaceous (DE), Comet(r), medicated bath powder, talcum powder or medicated skin powder into the crevices and cracks around baseboards.

It doesn't matter what you do, just remember to minimize clutter. Continue to caulk. And clean regularly. Store everything possible in plastic or airtight storage containers and continue to vacuum until the bedbugs are all gone. Bed bug infestations can be vacuumed with the help of a special attachment. Vacuum baseboards along with nearby furniture such as bedstands, rails headboards foot boards and bed seams. Also vacuum along carpet edges as well (especially the tack stripes). To remove bed bugs, it's best to scrape the edge of the vacuum attachment across the infested area. It is best to avoid using a brush attachment, as this could spread the bed bug infestation to different areas. You can remove your bedbugs, their eggs and all dirt by thoroughly vacuuming all hiding spots on a regular basis. Launder all linens in borax every other week. You will need to monitor the home until no bed bugs or eggs are found. The bed and soft furnishings should be vacuumed daily. Also, check all drawers and cabinets. This should be done in an organized, careful manner. Make sure to vacuum every part of the room. You can use a dry vacuum if you don't want to wet it with water. Add some food-grade DE talcum powder before starting. Pour your rinse-and -vac in the toilet. Flush. Using a Steam cleaner, steam those exact areas. Caulk or seal all cracks, crevices, and holes around walls and flooring. You can use bed bug interception devices or monitors to check for signs of active infestation. Regularly use diluted enzyme cleaners that contain peppermint.

BED BUG TREATMENT 3. Sealants

Close or seal mattresses, pillows, and box springs completely. This prevents bed bugs and dust mites from infesting. It also helps to reduce pet dander. If you don't have bedbugs, dust mites will still be present in your home ---- wherever there are warm temperatures and humidity. It is best to keep them indoors as they are able to feed on dead skin and mold spores. About 200,000 asthmatics visit the ER each year due to dust mites. Dust mite bed bug and dust mite covers work well to keep them at bay. According to one study, children with allergies to dust mites who use dust mite bed and pillow covers can reduce the amount of medicine they take by half. Their mattresses were tested and dust mites colony numbers decreased. In mattress or allergy supply shops, you can buy dust mite protectors for your mattresses, pillows and boxes springs. These covers come in many different types of material.

With zippers or covers in vinyl, you can seal allergens in and prevent inhalation.

The covers of vinyl and plastic are much easier to clean compared with those made of natural materials.

To make plastic covers more comfortable, many of them have an outer material such as nylon.

As soon as you get your pillows and mattresses, try to protect them.

Cover zippers with duct tape, electrical tape or both to prevent dust mites, bed bugs or other insects from getting in.

BED BUG TREATMENT #4. DUSTING WITH DIATOMACEOUS FOOD GRADE EARTHE

It is made from natural substances that are beneficial to animals, pets and livestock.

You can use diatomaceous to remove worms as well as parasites. Food-grade DE kills pests either by blocking their spiracles or by drying them out. However, we can consume it without any harm. DE kills insects by either sucking them up or scouring away their exoskeleton with abrasive force. This is different from synthetic pesticides. Synthetic pesticides rely on volatile and hazardous poisons. Bed bugs and other pests can be controlled without dangerous pesticides. It is not possible for insects to become resistant to the physical control, but it can happen with synthetic and volatile chemical POISONS. Please see http://www.safesolutionsinc.com/ on how to order. Be careful not to use too much DE. Bed bugs can be controlled by dusting the bed first, and covering the mattress. Powder can be sprinkled lightly around furniture, beds and carpets. It is not toxic and can be used in organic feed for both livestock and animals. However, bed bugs will not survive.

If you want to keep bed bugs off your mattress, use this DE powder in 4 non-breakable cup or caps. Place the bed legs inside.

The use of organic agriculture and gardening is not safe with all forms diatomaceous soil (DE). DE, which is commonly used to filter swimming pools is harmful for humans and won't control bugs. DE products marketed as "insecticides" are often laced with chemicals like piperonyl-butoxide or pyrethrum. They should not be fed to either animals or people. Safe Solutions DE has a Food Grade quality and is made from non-contaminated deposits of fresh water.

DE (Food-Grade DE) is a flour made of diatoms. Microscopically small fossils found in water deposit are ground to make DE. Diatoms - tiny, single-celled algae and plankton - are found in oceans by the billions. They form the base of marine food chains. Without diatoms, even great whales would not be able to survive. When diatoms die their exoskeletons sink to the bottom and build up diatomaceous deposits over time. As geological changes occur, these sea sediments are slowly shifted onto dry land. They can now be mined. Due to water currents many deposits can become unclean, and some may even contain arsenic. This is dangerous. Safe Solutions DE originates from fresh-water deposits which are 100% safe and non-toxic.

It was the Author's friend, who had brought bedbugs back from an overseas trip. Recalling a lecture he heard about how fine dust would smother insect pests, he decided to use his wife's bath-powder that same night. Use respirator, dust gently and evenly all surfaces in affected rooms, including bed frames and mattresses. This includes folds, edges, cracks, crevices, etc. Spread fine body wash powder liberally on the two sides of the bed frame and gently work into it. The bed bugs in your mattress should vanish over night. You can cover the mattress in a plastic sheet before using it to sleep again.

BED BUG TRAP #5. BEDBUG STRAINS AND TAPES

If you are inspecting for bed bugs, duct-tape can be used to install sticky sides upwards to trap them. If you want to keep bedbugs out of corners or power outlets or clothes or furniture that is upholstered, use packing tape or good quality duct tap. When using duct tap, make sure to use masking or scotch tape. Many commercial bed bug traps that are sold on the market use CO2 and can be as expensive as $600. But you can easily make your traps yourself for less.

Use duct-tape with sticky-side-up to surround the heating pad. Place fresh bean-leaves or several glue-boards or sticky-traps on top of the heating pad. Let the pad run all night and lower the temperature. You can check in the morning for bed bugs that may have been trapped by the glue or the new bean leaves. Improve the trap by placing an Alka Seltzer tablet onto a dampened sponge placed on a tiny plate over the heating pad. It is important that the tablet dissolves slowly.

The materials needed for making great interception bed bugs traps

Two-liter bottles

Bottle of 50 gm Brown Sugar

Bottle contains 1 gram (0.035-ounce) yeast

Thermometer

Measurement cup

Knifes and sharp scissors

Chapter 5: The Fabric Is Non-Woven

Instructions:

Cut the bottle tops off where they start to turn-in. This will allow the tops to be later inverted and used as funnels. For each trap: Pour one cup warm water in another container. Stir in two ounces of sugar. As soon as the water cools down, wait until it reaches 120 degrees F (40 degrees C). Once the sugar liquid has cooled to 40 degrees C or 120 degrees F, you can add one gram yeast into each bottle. As the sugar liquids cool, they will trigger yeast and create carbon dioxide. The gas will then attract blood suckers like bed bugs, fleas and ticks. You can use the bottom part to funnel the liquid into the bottles. Apply Vaseline and tape the new outer edges. You can cover the outside surfaces of bottles and tape with non-woven or cloth. You can place the traps anywhere you see recent bed bug activity. Every two weeks, empty the traps and refill the solution into the toilet.

Use talcum, Vaseline (petroleum jelly) or double-sided carpeting tape to coat the bottom of the bed's legs. Just place the duct-tape with its sticky side upwards around the mattress, bed legs and surrounding room. Use masking tape to secure it. As bedbugs cannot easily climb metal or polished glass surfaces, place the metal cap or glass jar of each leg in a glass jar. Lightly dust with Food-grade De. Don't let the covers of the mattress touch the wall or ground. Sticky-side-up, duct tape can be used to check for bedbug infestation.

BED BUG TREATMENT #6 UV LIGHTS

It is possible for a bed bug to survive 16 months in a mattress. It is a good idea to regularly disinfect bedding and the mattress with ultraviolet light. Nano UV (TM), disinfection wand and scanner, are small and light-weight disinfection products that utilize ultra-violet radiation to destroy germs from surface infections, as well as eggs and lice of fleas. The surfaces will be

99.99% virus and germ free in just 10 seconds! Kills Eschericichia Coli (E--Coli), Staphylococcus albus, Staphylococcus aureus, Salmonella.,B. Parathphosus, Corynebacterium diphtheriae , Eberthella typhosa, Dysentery bacili, Streptococcus hemolyticus Asian Bird Flu and the Eggs.

It is important to note that, in addition these UV lights, the sun can be used for a short time. Dust mites will survive wash cycles and dryer cycles. However, they won't be able to endure sunlight or ultraviolet light.

BED BUG TREATMENT #7.TWEETMINT ENZYME CLEANER WITH PEPPERMINT

Tweetmin Enzyme Cleaner with Peppermint is the perfect all-natural pesticide (see: http://www.theidealpesticide.com). This is a safe and effective enzyme cleaner that contains peppermint (salt), dish soap, protease enzymes (meat tenderizer) and glycerin. Most people use this product to regularly clean and they find there are no bugs. The Author patents the use of enzymes to effectively and safely kill most insects and arachnids. It also controls fungus mold mildew bacteria viruses and arachnids. Please see:

Insects also use protease to molt, so they can never become resistant to this perfect pesticide. As insects also use the protease-enzymes to molt they cannot become resistant. The Author has patented a non-toxic formulation that can either be mopped over or sprayed onto the bed bug infestation, including beds, mattresses bedding, furniture walls ceilings flooring, clothes, luggage, and even on clothing. Safe Solutions Tweetmint Enzme Cleaner Peppermint literally melts exoskeletons of bed bugs and can kill them on direct contact. Don't you already feel better thinking of it?

Your bed bug control options

Sun Tzu stated in the "Art of War" book that understanding our enemy was essential to victory. Sun Tzu further wrote, "When our enemy is relaxed we should make him work." Once they have eaten, force them to starve. If they have settled down, then make them go. "--"Knowing your opponent and knowing yourself will keep you safe in any battle. Knowing yourself but not the enemy gives you equal chances to win or lose. When you're ignorant of both your enemy and self, it is certain that every battle will end in disaster. "--"Being unprepared is the biggest crime. Being prepared for every contingency in advance is the best virtue. "--"So, war-trained soldiers can conquer the enemy's armies without any battle .... They win by using strategy. And "In war, the speed of action is crucial: You cannot afford to ignore opportunities." In order to avoid bedbug infestations in the first place, the author recommends that you choose the safest method possible.

Bed bug control options are available to you. It is obvious that your enemy bed bug has a much more sophisticated and well-prepared opponent. In order to avoid bed bugs invading your office or home, you should remove all conditions that could lead to infestation, i.e. by first caulking. There are many options available if bed bug infestations occur. Simply dusting the bed, and placing a mattress protector on it can be effective in destroying all your bed bug enemy. If you want to prevent further infestations of bed bugs, it is best that you inspect and dust your bed every day, regularly clean the area with enzymes and peppermint cleaners or use UV light or heat treatment. In the event that your bed bug enemy invades and takes over large portions of your home or business, then you'll need to try a variety of combinations from Author's alternate controls. The combination of bed bug dusts or mattress covers with UV spot treatment, vacuuming, dusting, monitoring and cleaning will be necessary. The mere act of hiring a company to be your mercenary does not stop bed bug re-infestations. Be sure to fully accept and understand the various contract and control clauses of any pest control service you hire.

The most important aspect of any war, however, is the victory.

Chapter 6: Bed Bug Information And History

"Why do I need to know about the history of bed bugs?" you might ask.

I'd like nothing more to provide you with the initial phase of the treatment procedure immediately. But, you'll need an understanding of bed bugs so that you can build an understanding base of the process that lies in the future. Imagine the event as one that is a sports competition. It is essential to establish an attitude to beat your adversaries. In this article, I'll provide an in-depth look at bed bugs to help you know what you're up against, and what is necessary to do to prevail.

Bed bugs aren't a modern phenomenon that is being hyped up in the media. They've been in existence for many thousands of years. There is evidence to suggest that the Romans as well as the ancient Egyptians were plagued by bed bugs.

Bed bug infestations aren't uncommon to America and are not a new phenomenon. It is believed that they hitched travel with colonists back in the 17th century, on their travels over into the Atlantic Ocean.

Bed bugs flourished throughout America in the 1950s until they became nearly extinct due to the use of highly poisonous pesticides. But, these chemicals can are serious dangers for the human health and environment as well as new rules concerning pesticides have significantly restricted their use over the last few years.

When toxic chemicals were removed, the bed bug population returned in a big way and thrive throughout the world. In addition to the need for restrictions on the use of insecticides that are dangerous There are many other reasons that are responsible for the rise of bed bug.

* Even if the effective pesticides were not banned through laws, they were getting

more and less effective due to the fact that bed bugs acquired tolerance to their use. Bed bugs have become resistant to the majority of current insecticides and pesticides.

* Bed bugs are skilled travelers who hide behind bags and clothes, giving their passengers free access to any region of the world with the advent of global travel.

* Bed bugs reproduce rapidly and are able to create large numbers that are not detected for significant periods of time.

Many people have no idea of bed bugs because they are ignorant or have no knowledge about bed bugs.

* Prior to a few years ago the majority of people, including professional pest control experts--had little experience with dealing with bed bug infestations.

* Up to now, we aren't taking the problem seriously as a whole.

Will We Win Against Bed Bugs?

Bed bugs have become sufficient of a concern within America. United States that they have Americans pay attention to, but the issue has now become obvious to all that the need for a large-scale, effective solution to this issue is required. The various levels of the government, researchers and pest control firms as well as travel and hospitality industry are coming together in order to solve the problem.

Yet, many people don't have the necessary knowledge and skills to address the problem their own. To make things worse it appears that the hotel and travel industry seems to put an emphasis in a way on reaction tactics rather than prevention. I am concerned about this.

I am convinced that we will begin fighting the battle against bed bugs when the focus is on preventing bed bugs from taking their footholds initially. In the meantime, we're obliged to engage in defensive tactics to fight the bugs off. In the end, however I believe that the problem of bed bugs across the United States will continue to become worse in the coming time.

Chapter 7: The Psychological And Emotional Effects Of Bed Bugs

Bed bugs are famous because of their bites. They also cause the greatest damage via emotional and mental traumas. What could be more painful than being attacked within the area where you're supposed to feel most safe?

When bed bugs invade your bedroom, you'll find that your evenings are unable to sleep and plagued by anxiety and fear. Each night, stress increases in a way that has a cumulative effect comparable to - and even more severe than - post-traumatic anxiety disorder. If you permit them to persist, they can last for a long time after insects have gone.

Keep Your Head Up

It is a fact that every person who has left their house is susceptible to an infestation of bed bugs. The cleanliness and status of the home are not the only factors. Keep your head high and address this issue with a straight face. There's no reason to feel ashamed about the fact for the fact that bed bugs have chosen your place of residence. They're not a particular species. They'll be anywhere, no matter if they're welcomed or not.

Maintain Control of Your Life

These tips will assist you keep control of your daily life when you're struggling with bed bugs:

Be aware of the situation. Being faced with a bedbug problem can be a daunting experience. Be reminded often that this is just a temporary issue and a stage of your life.

Make sure you are diligent with your efforts to get rid of the clutter as well as following the directions that are in the book with care. If you are able to see your improvement, your perception of the situation is likely to change.

Don't isolate you or your family members.

* Utilize your support network. Speak about your concerns to people you trust can aid you in coping your stress and anxiety.

The best way to protect yourself is to speak truthfully with relatives and friends. It will help them safeguard themselves, and stop the spread of an infection into their homes.

Make sure you get outside and have fun. You must find things that let your mind unwind.

Do not hesitate to reach out for assistance.

Do Not Allow Fear to Control You

Sometimes, physically eliminating bed bugs is not the only part of the fight. If you're experiencing mental and psychological issues which affect your daily life, you should seek out professional counselling. I've heard from many people who have found that talking to a professional was beneficial for their lives. If you do not own insurance coverage, your physician may refer you to an organization which will offer services at free or in a scale that is sliding. I understand the strain and inconvenience that bed bugs result in. But, I can assure you that you'll be able to be able to enjoy your life once more.

If the situation is severe, individuals report suffering from major depression and suicidal thoughts. If you feel self-harming or contemplating self-harm, you should visit an emergency room or consult a medical professional right away. Be aware that it's okay to seek assistance. It is also possible to contact for help the National Suicide Prevention Lifeline at 1-800-273-TALK.

Chapter 8: Should I Really Do This Myself?

Two quotes on "half measures" that I have come to love through my own life. I use their concept for every goal that I have set to achieve. The first quote comes taken from The Alcoholics Anonymous Big Book:

"Half measures didn't help us. The moment we stood was the pivot moment."

When it comes to critical situations in critical situations, half-measures yield no results. This is particularly true in the case of treating bed bugs. 100% of your dedication and determination will be needed to bring to the point which you're at now.

The third quote comes the one I use from my most cherished television shows, Breaking Bad. The character in the show is fictional. Mike Ehrmantraut, head of security for corporate in Los Pollos Hermanos, is talking to Walter White about his past wrongdoings:

"I took a half-measure instead of going full-on. I'll never make the same error ever again. There will be no more half measures. Walter."

(Jonathan Banks) and Bryan Cranston are the actors who played the characters in the show.)

I'm not looking to spend your time on something that isn't important So why do I talk about movies and quotes? It's because I believe that it's vital that you comprehend and embrace the mentality necessary to accomplish the job in front of you.

As long as you're determined to follow the complete methods described in this guide You are equipped to eliminate bed bugs for yourself.

Chapter 9: Verifying A Bed Bug Infestation (The Initial Inspection)

A third of those who have been attacked by bed bugs don't show obvious signs that they have been bitten. Additionally, there can be several symptoms of other insect bites as well as allergens, bacteria and other insects which could appear to be bed bites.

So, don't rely on bite marks or their absence to determine the presence of the presence of bed bugs.

Excrement, Blood Spots, and Eggs

The most reliable method to determine whether you have the presence of an infestation is to look for evidence of the insects the bugs. Utilize a magnifying device along with the ultraviolet (UV) illumination source look for signs of the excrement of bed bugs as well as blood spots and eggs.

If you are suffering from an infestation, you'll most likely see eggs, blood spots and other signs.

The bed bug's feces may look like a small, shadow about the width of the beginning sentence.

* The blood spots will appear as tiny blood spots caused by crushed bed bugs that have landed on your mattress or bedding.

Eggs appear clear or white, and are approximately the same size the excrement. (2-3mm of length)

Image uploaded by Flickr user Louento.Pix (CC BY-ND 2.0)

These signs can be helpful to verify the situation but none of them is 100% reliable when it comes to finding a bedbug infestation. These signs might be an entirely different type of or even more so, this information alone could cause one to believe you are experiencing a bedbug presence.

Skin Castings and Live Bed Bugs

To ensure confidence, confirm the presence of bed bugs by looking for the live bed bug as well as skin castings. Bed bugs make castings of their skins every time they expand. The castings can vary a amount in their size, however they are easy to spot these castings. They appear like an imitation of live bugs.

Image taken by the flickr user Louento.Pix (CC BY-ND 2.0)

What Do Bed Bugs Look Like?

Adults:

Bed bugs that are adults tiny oval-shaped bugs, with antennae and six legs.

* Prior to feeding, they are about 5- 6mm (about 1/8 inch) in length. They are flat-looking and have a reddish-brown color.

Following a meal after a meal, they grow by 7-10mm (about 3/8 of an inch) in length and then turn in red.

Image created by user on flickr Louento.Pix (CC BY-ND 2.0)

Youth:

* Nymphs (juveniles) vary in size between 1mm and 4mm (barely apparent to the size of 1/8 of an inch).

* Before feeding, the color is a light whitish-transparent.

Then, after feeding, Nymphs change to a vibrant blood red.

Identification Tips

It is essential to look at the most photos you can in order to get familiar with the look and appearance of the bed bug. Make use of the sources included in this article, as well as further online photos. Other online resources, such as:

While observing bed bug infestations by yourself, or snapping a picture for posting on Reddit.com the best option is to put the bug on a clear or smooth surface in order in order to make it easier to identify its traits simpler. The photos taken from the side, the bottom and top sides, with sufficient lighting is also beneficial when you post to reddit.com to confirm.

Equipment like a flashlight or magnifying glass can make the identification process easier.

Other Bugs and Items That Are Commonly Mistaken for Bed Bugs

What makes identifying bed bugs even difficult is the fact that all bugs appear alike in appearance. They are nitty bits of junk found within their homes. Here's a list of the most common objects and bugs that are often mistaken for bed bugs, their nymphs, as well as their eggs.

* Bat bugs

* Spider beetle

*Tick bugs

* The larva of the Larder Beetle

* Juvenile German cockroaches

* Dried skin

* Dried nasal mucus

* Seeds, pebbles, as well as other tiny bits of dirt

Where to Look

Bed bugs are known to move up to 20 feet away from their homes for food. The majority of infestations are found in the vicinity of beds. Be aware that bed bugs could easily get into tiny hiding areas. If you are able to slip the edges of your credit card through the crevice or crack in your wall the area is big enough to house bed bugs.

You should focus your efforts in the seams and crevices of the mattress or box spring.

The other areas to look at are (but don't limit yourself to):

* Seams and tags on boxes springs and mattresses.

Cracks, crevices as well as screw holes on the headboard, bed frame and the walls around the mattress

* Seams and folds for couch cushions, chairs and curtains

* Furniture joints like on a night stand

* Appliances inside

* Picture frames

* Receptacles for electrical power

* Carpet seams at the point where the floor and wall meet.

Drywall seams are between ceilings and walls

Chapter 10: Determining The Extent Of The Infestation (The Full Inspection)

The most frequent causes of failures in control when dealing with bed bugs is the inability to thoroughly inspect and locate all bugs in their hiding spots. The aim of an extensive inspection is to obtain crucial details about the location as well as the severity of the presence. This data will be extremely beneficial in the subsequent measures to treat.

Take note of where in your home are you more often getting bitten, and also where you've seen bed bugs. Consider your movement and sleep patterns. If you've slept across different areas of your house, each of those areas needs to be examined and addressed.

The University of Kentucky conducted a study to find out the most likely places to see bed bugs within your house. The percentages below are intended for educational purpose only. Every space and every pest is unique.

These findings are based upon an investigation of 13 homes that were infested by bed bugs. The bed bugs were identified:

* 34.6 percent - box spring

* 22.6 percent of furniture including sofas and chairs with upholstered cushions

* 22.4% - mattress

* 13.4 percent of headboard and bed frame

* 3.1 percentage - area of the baseboard

* 2.3 percent ceilings and walls

* 1.4 percent. Other

* .2 percent - nightstands and dressers

The Inspection Process

Bed bugs possess a rectangular body that allows they to conceal themselves in every crack and crevice. They are attracted to darkness, isolation, and secure areas. they are fond of papers, wood and even fabric, so take extra care of the area and materials.

Check your mattress first, and pay close focus on the following places:

* Seams

* Labels

* Corner guards

* Beading

* Buttons

Be sure to inspect the components that are adjacent for example:

* Casters with hollow plastic legs

* Coils for bed springs

* The interiors of posts for beds.

* Bedframe

* Headboard

* If your bed is made of wooden slats that are inspected, you should check each one carefully. wooden slats have many cracks where bed bugs could conceal and lay their eggs.

• If the slats of wood were fastened to the bedframe the bolts must be removed and the holes in which they were drilled examined and then treated.

If the bed you are using is one that is an assembly bed you should inspect your bed's base for bugs as it's more likely to contain bugs.

Make sure you check the edge of the piece beneath the base of the ensemble.

The bed's surrounding areas must be examined further:

The bedside furniture like furniture, cabinets, and other furniture must be examined and turned.

The drawers on the furniture in your bed are to be removed and checked.

* If headboards are affixed on the walls, they need to be removed in order to provide access to inspect and treat.

After you've thoroughly examined the mattress, proceed to check the rest of the room, examining the furniture and other objects across the space with a keen eye on the seams, buttons, and areas made of wood. Below is a list of items that are often overlooked and places:

* Luggage

* Places in which luggage is located.

* Devices like telephones and alarm clocks as well as other.

* Books

* Laundry and clothes (both both dirty and clean)

* Under switch plates, and outlets for electrical power

* Smoke detectors

* Light fittings

* Underneath carpet edges

* Door transitions under the floor

* Underneath rugs

* Skirting boards. Joins to floor boards

* Wall paper that is loose and paint

* Old screw and nail holes in ceilings and walls

* Walls and ceilings

* All other walls that are not void

* Moldings

* Window casings

* Mirrors, frames for pictures or the rest of your wall hangings

Maintain records of the places where bed bugs are active. The majority of bed bug prevention guidelines advise you to examine the rooms adjacent to, above or beneath the area where there is an outbreak. I would suggest that you inspect the entire home. There is no reason to use only a small amount in the event that you have to take the whole way. If you can identify all the harborages Control and treatment can be much easier and successful.

High-Risk Factors That Could Affect Your Treatment Efforts

A variety of risk factors that can be found on the spot of the infection can make treatment extremely difficult and can increase the risk of failure in treatment. They include:

*Clutter The control of bed bugs with a messy home is virtually impossible. If you're surrounded by a lot of mess, I'll help you decide how to organize it into the next chapter.

* Collaboration: It is your responsibility to make sure that the other inhabitants of your household are aware that a the successful treatment of bed bugs is dependent on the cooperation of all members. It also requires cooperation from an owner if you're renting, as well as the cooperation of neighbors when you reside in a multi occupancy house.

* Room integrity and construction Some building materials, like exposed brick can create the most difficult conditions for treatment. Additionally, gaps that are too large or cracks and crevices between walls and ceilings, floors, trimming, and moldings are all likely to make eliminating bed bugs harder.

Multi-Unit Dwellings: Treatment of Duplexes, apartments, as well as condominiums can be more difficult due to the greater probability of having to re-infest the property.

* High Infestations: Higher infestations are likely to require additional treatments and more time.

Incorrect Control Methods You have tried to eliminate the bed bug issue applying improper techniques to manage the infestation There is a high likelihood that you caused the problem to get more difficult by bringing the pest to the extent that it encroached on your property. A few exterminators are not willing to do the work in the event of evidence showing that the method you employed was not properly designed like the use of a "bug bomb." Another method to make the situation worse is attempt to eradicate bed bug infestations using your vacuum cleaner before creating proper containment for your room in addition to following the directions in this book. Do things in a step-by-step manner and you'll get better outcomes.

Prepare for Treatment: Chapter 6I urge you gather the necessary supplies before treating the infestation. It is best to prepare everything in advance so that you can move seamlessly from one treatment to another. The success of the treatments will depend on this.

It may be necessary to repeat certain actions. Bed bugs cannot be eliminated by a single, quick product or treatment. A multi-pronged approach is the only way to be successful. You shouldn't worry if there are still signs of bed bugs even after you follow these simple steps. Don't forget that your treatment method gives you the upper hand. You are also several steps away from getting rid of bedbugs for good.

The following is a checklist of items that you need before beginning the battle. You'll learn where and when to use each item in the following chapters. It is important that you read the whole guide, before beginning any step. That way you will have a clear picture of all you need to do. You might find out that, depending upon your specific situation, some of the items below in the list you can skip.

This list may look overwhelming at first. Nevertheless, it is important to note that bed bug treatment costs can start at as little as $1,000 or as much as $2,000. They may even go as high as $6000 to $7000 dollars. It is your responsibility, not the pest control company, to prepare and administer supplemental treatment. The majority of these expenses would be incurred even if you hire an exterminator.

This book contains a list of all these products. They are all discussed in detail in the Bed Bug Supply Manual which is included as part of your purchase.

Bed Bug Supply Manual explains each item I've used. It also tells you where to buy it quickly and at a low cost. Many of these items are already present in your household. Many of them are available in your local store. Some may have to be ordered. Bed Bug Supply Manual helps you to figure out all this information.

If you are in a position where you simply cannot afford any other supplies, there are some frugal options. These alternatives are explained in great detail in the Bed Bug Supply Manual. The Bed Bug Supply Manual is a free resource that explains these alternative methods in detail. I'm not recommending all of them, but i still offer them. I think it's best to choose a less expensive and more effective method than to completely skip part of the treatment. The lack of cash should not be a reason to avoid getting rid or bed bugs. I strive to make sure that everyone can find solutions. Bed Bug Supply Manual gives you an idea which alternative you are able to use, and those you need to stay away from.

List of Supplies

* Thick garbage bags (contractor bags)

Ziploc(r), a resealable bag, is available in both 2.5 gallon and 1 gallon.

* Vacuum cleaners with hose

Bucket

* Dish detergent

The Sponge

* Use Lysol(r), or other strong cleaning products

Each boxspring or mattress affected by the flood zone will require a mattress encasement.

* Pillow covers

Caulk gun with a few paintable tubes of latex caulk

* Climb up bed bug interceptors

* Joint compound

* Wood filler if necessary

* Expanding Foam (if necessary)

• Utility knife

You can also use paper towels.

CimeXa® or another 100% amorphous, silica gel-based desiccant is included in the package.

* Pest control duster

The tape can be either three to four rolls transparent packaging tape (such as Scotch® tape) or three to four rolls transparent adhesive with a flat surface. It is better to use packing tape, though either will work.

Steam cleaner

It is important to have white linens. This includes white bed sheets, pillow cases and cotton blankets. Cotton sheets and cotton quilts are both easily washable and dryable. The comforters themselves may still harbor bedbugs even after they have been dried.

Duct tape

Murphy's Oil Soap, for wooden bedframes. This is a good contact killer and can be used to clean wood.

Optional Items

The following are some of the topics you will learn about later.

Mineral oil

The petroleum jelly Vaseline (r) and other similar products

* Pesticide

Disposable laundry Bags

Chapter 11: The Importance Of Containment

You should now protect your bed. This guide shows you how. It will also provide immediate relief for you and your family from the bed bug bites.

Most pest control professionals argue that bed bugs will continue to consume you alive if you leave the mattress unprotected. It is believed that they do so to stop the bugs from spreading and to limit the size of the infestation. This is easy to say for them! The people who suffer from insomnia and no hope of relief are not the ones that they blame.

It is here that this bed bug control plan stands out from all the other plans I have come across. Although I'm not convinced bed bugs are going to flee from your bedroom just because your bed is protected, it doesn't mean they will. It is possible that they will still try to leave the treated area when we perform other pest management procedures.

The first step involves trapping or killing bed bugs when they try to climb onto your bed. The first step is to trap or kill bed bugs as they climb up your bed. To prevent bed bugs from escaping, you should take precautions to avoid them coming into contact with any other treatment method.

It is easy for bedbugs to move between rooms through small cracks. To eliminate their entry and exit routes, we need to block off the paths. In a unit that is attached to another, such as a townhouse or apartment, you must stop the pests from going to and fro. The adjacent dwellings increase your risk of being infected and even getting reinfested, after you have successfully treated the infestation.

These instructions will help you to prevent an infestation from spreading.

Things You Will Need

The tape should be transparent with a totally smooth surface. Scotch® tape (the shiny type) is a good alternative.

* CimeXa (silica gel desiccant dust). Since I've been using silica dust desiccant for many years now, instead of diatomaceous soil which worked well over the past few decades. All the benefits of diatomaceous soil are achieved with this dust, but it is quicker and easier. This product is safe, but also inexpensive.

* Pest control duster. This product may have to be ordered on-line. The local stores did not have one. In the event that you are unable to find a duster you could use an empty bottle of squeeze. This won't be as effective, but will still allow you to finish your task without any delay. Wearing a goggle and mask during the application is recommended if your pest-control duster has been replaced by a squeeze spray.

The Advantages of 100% Amorphous Silica Dust over Diatomaceous Earth

The most important part of any treatment is the 100% ASG desiccant. This dust can also be called "ASG dust", "100% ASG" or "desiccant". Hereafter, it will be referred to as "ASG powder."

ASG powder is made synthetically by mixing sand with a few simple ingredients. It is not gel despite the term "silica gel". The substance is hard and is often formed into dust or beads. As the name implies, it is not crystalline. That's why humans and other animals can safely use this material. The synthetic forms of amorphous silicon gel are often used as drying or anti-clumping agent in powdered products such as cosmetics, pharmaceuticals and foods.

ASG Dust is better at attracting bed bugs than diatomaceous soil because ASG dust has an adhesive effect. It is important to use very thin dust layers in order for bed bugs not be deterred. The bedbugs will not come in contact with the dust when it's applied thickly. The dust quickly attaches itself to their body and absorbs any protective covering. They will die within 24 to 48 hours.

ASG dust not only kills bed bugs better than any diatomaceous soil, it is safer. As an example, ASG dust is safe to use on open surfaces, while diatomaceous eagle can only be used for cracks or crevices. ASG contains less crystallized silicon than diatomaceous Earth, which can cause lung damage or inhalation hazards. ASG dust will be discussed in more detail later.

Build a barrier to protect rooms from bed bugs

Get started!

To begin, you will need to place a bed bug barrier around the rooms that were infested. Use ASG dust along with smooth

Scotch or clear packaging tape to make this barrier.

1. The dust should be applied around the perimeter of a room at the point where the edge of carpeting or the floor meets the wall. It is best to use a fine, light dusting. As the primary purpose is to form a protective barrier, it's okay to apply more to all surfaces. You should not overdo it at this stage because you don't want to just prevent bugs from coming into contact with it.

You'll also want to apply a fine dusting in every crack or crevice. We will cover this topic later on. As of now, you should focus on "containment" by creating a barrier around the perimeters of the room.

A pest control duster is the best way to use ASG. This pest control tool is inexpensive and does an even better job of applying the ASG dust than does a standard squeeze bottle. You can apply it in places that are difficult to reach. You can squeeze bottles in an emergency, but you'll have trouble getting the right amount of dust, covering the area, and distributing it to hard-to reach areas. A good duster will save you frustration, and help to avoid a less-than-perfect job.

2. ASG Dust can also be used to cover areas around doors that would otherwise not be accessible with a duster. Because it has static, this dust will adhere to many vertical surfaces. It is important to stop bed bugs using walls or ceilings to travel from room-to-room through middle and top doorways.

3. ASG dust is a better option than sealing or caulking cracks, crevices and voids along the perimeter of a room. The bed bugs will continue to hide in these places for as long as they want. That way, there is less chance of them spreading and contaminating other things or rooms.

4. Apply a horizontal layer 6-12 inch above the bottom of the baseboard, of clear packaging tape. Because bed bugs' claws cannot grab smooth surfaces like drywall, this tape acts as another barrier. Make sure that you go all around the room to make sure there aren't any gaps. Make sure you check to see how many inches of tape is included with each package. This will help you determine how much to use to cover your entire room. It is best to tape as many walls as you can, without breaking the tape. Two people can help with this step.

Once you have reached a threshold, turn the tape 90 degrees to the vertical and continue around the whole door. It will prevent bedbugs from climbing up the wall or the ceiling to reach the doorway. ASG dust can be added to the trim at the top of your door for additional protection.

If you want to, repeat the same process in a horizontal pattern around the area where the ceiling meets the wall. Although it's rare, bedbugs have fallen from the ceiling on to beds.

5. The same type of barrier can be used in adjacent rooms which may also have an infestation. It will all depend on how you inspect the room. It is possible for some people to create a perimeter around only one space. It may be necessary to place a barrier in every room.

Ch. 9: Is it better to "protect" or isolate your bed?

One of the most heated debates between pest control specialists is whether to isolate beds or protect them from bed bugs.

What Is Bed Protection?

Bed bugs can be found in bedframes, headboards, and mattresses. In order to protect your beds, you should encase the mattresses and box springs with high-quality bed bug-proof covers. The bed bug will still be capable of crawling on the mattress to bite, but by taking these steps you can ensure that they won't be able stay in your bed. If you are able to gain some comfort from the knowledge that they may not be able to survive in your bed if you treat their barriers, you can enjoy knowing they have eaten their last meal.

Protecting the bed may sound better than isolating because it won't prevent them from ever biting you. They will bite you less, but still gain access. You can still grit your teeth, but you will have a better chance of success.

What Is Bed Isolation?

It means taking the steps necessary to remove them from your bed. Then, take further steps to stop them getting back. Some professionals in pest control are not fans of this solution. Others believe it would be a mistake to fully isolate the mattress because they will spread and disperse.

Many professionals suggest that you should isolate.

What Method Should I Choose?

What's my take? I believe the debate will continue to rage for years.

You can isolate your bedroom, but I suggest that you protect it.

If you are bitten by bedbugs in bed and find evidence of them, you will know that there is still an infestation. Your home needs further treatment. Bed isolation can make it harder to confirm if the bed bug infestation is still there, especially if your body does not react to the bites that you receive during the night.

If you've followed this guide to this point you should have enough information on how to contain the area around your room. (See Chapter 7). I will then describe more techniques in the chapter following. The process is not affected by whether your bed is isolated or not.

A strong argument could be made to say that by being able to quickly detect and monitor bed bugs during subsequent treatment phases, which bed protection allows, but bed isolation doesn't, you will have a more effective and quicker removal. When you isolate your bed, the bugs will return. If you fail to catch them during initial treatments, then you can easily detect and eliminate the problem. The bugs stop nipping at you immediately when you're sleeping in bed isolation. But you may lose sleep due to anxiety.

Why would You choose to isolate your mattress?

When you experience severe pain, an allergic reaction, emotional distress or mental turmoil, it is okay to separate your bed. This will not affect the treatment. This is a good option, but you'll need to double-check that your containment zones are solid. This will prevent bedbugs from spreading through your house. Just ensure that you spread ASG dust evenly around the border of the area so that bed bug can contact it from all angles. So long as the containment zones are maintained, bed bugs have no place to hide or run.

Chapter 12: Treatment For The Bed

After deciding whether to isolate your bed from others or just protect it, your next steps are the same. Both methods will require that you eliminate all bed bugs in the bed, including the mattress, headboard and boxspring. Next, cover your bed and its boxspring.

You will all need:

You can also buy encasements to protect your mattress, pillow, and box spring.

* New pillows

*White sheets, white pillows cases and white cotton covers. Cotton sheets and blankets can be washed easily and dried quickly, however comforters could harbor bed bugs after drying for an extended period of time.

* High-quality duct taping

* Contractor thick bags

Ziploc storage bags are available in 2.5 and 5 gallon sizes.

Murphy's Oil Soap, for wood bedframes. Murphy's has been proven to be an effective bed bug contact killer and also works well for disinfecting wood.

ASG dust can also be referred to by the brand CimeXa or as 100% Amorphous Silica Gel desiccant. For more details on ASG, see Chapter 13

Steam cleaner

The following will be needed if you want to isolate your bed.

Bed-raisers, which raises the bed to prevent bedding from touching floors

Mineral Oil

Vaseline

Under the bed frame's legs, place 4 solid bowls (or bed bug interceptors) to hold mineral oil.

No matter if you want to protect your bed, or isolate it:

1. Stripe the bed. Tie a tight knot in the bag with all the dirty laundry. If the bag deflates when pushed, it is not airtight.

2. You should wash all your bedding right away. When opening the bags, be careful not to expose your laundry area to bed bugs. Bed Bug Supply Manual shows you how you can buy bags which dissolve in hot water and go directly into the machine.

3. The longest drying cycle is to use hot water for washing and high heat when drying. Two complete high-heat cycles may be required for heavy items in order to expose them to the temperature necessary. Once you have removed the clothing from the dryer and placed it into the new bag,

the bacteria will not be able to reinfest the garments.

4. Continue these steps after treating the bed to any curtains or clothing that you may have found in areas with infestations.

5. Reposition the bed frame away from a wall.

6. Box springs and mattresses should be thoroughly vacuumed.

You should read Chapter 11, which contains instructions for using a vacuum properly to get rid of bed bugs, their eggs and other pests.

It is important to vacuum the edge, seams, edges and surface of both the boxspring and mattress. Removing the dust covers on the underside of the mattress will reveal the framing. Bugs love this area to hide. Remove the dust cover from underneath the box spring to expose its framing. Bed bugs love this place. Be on the lookout for bed bug eggs at all times. It is here that a UV lamp will be extremely helpful, because eggs may not always be easy to identify due to the size or transparency. Since the egg shells are covered in an adhesive cement, a vacuum cleaner's suction is often not enough to get rid of all the eggs. To remove them, you'll have to scrape with the vacuum cleaner nozzle.

7. Vacuum bedframes and headboards. As the bedframes and headboards will not be covered, it is important to take special care of these areas. This is especially true for the bedframe as they often have numerous crevices or cracks that can allow critters to hide. Then, vacuum every crack and crevice. If you need full access to certain areas, you may have to completely disassemble the bedframe. ASG Dust or Steam can be used to treat all crevices and kill the bedbugs that are still present.

8. Wood filler or silicone caulk can be used to seal up the cracks and crevices. Apply it

to screw heads or other areas that you need for assembly and disassembly. You may have trouble if you decide to break down your bed at some stage, but it was not my primary concern.

9. Vacuum thoroughly under the bedframe and around it. The main thing to do is remove and destroy all bugs or eggs before installing encasements. Take special care to inspect seams, the ticking of your mattress, and any other voids.

10. In the case of a heavy infestation, ASG powder or steam can be applied to all bed component sections to eradicate any remaining bedbugs. The vacuuming is an optional part of the process. You can move to Step 11 if you feel that your bed has been cleaned enough.

If you are going to steam bed bugs, read up on the next section (Chapter 12.) in order to know how to do it properly.

To reduce the risk of mold, you should allow your mattress and boxspring to fully dry out before covering them.

11. Once your mattress has been treated, you can cover the entire mattress with mattress encasements. Although there are many different encasements on the market today, only a handful are effective against bedbugs. Bed Bug Supply Manual contains a listing of effective encasements against bedbugs. Encasements may be used on infected beds, or even to protect newer ones. If you install the encasements, all bugs or eggs still in your bed will eventually be killed by them.

12. You must be careful to not rip or tear the encasements when putting the mattress, box springs and frame back together. As encasements only work if they're intact, it's important to inspect them regularly to ensure that they aren’t ripped, torn and worn. Particularly vulnerable to damage are the parts of the encasement

that touch sharp protrusions such as the bolts in your bedframe or other edges. This can be increased by using duct-tape or some other type of cushioning over the affected areas.

13. Apply a light dusting around your bedposts if you choose to protect it rather than isolate it. Be careful to only use a small amount of ASG. If you are not going to isolate your bed you should use the ASG to dust the posts. If you don't dust lightly, your bed may end up "isolated".

You can isolate your bed by following these simple steps.

14. Place your bed on a riser to prevent your sheets, blankets and other bedding from touching the floor as you sleep.

15. Put mineral oil inside the solid bowls that you place under the bed's legs. Bed bugs trying to climb on the bed are trapped by the mineral oil.

16. Apply Vaseline to the top and bottom of the tape and wrap it around the legs. Vaseline, as well as the cellophane tape you use to wrap around legs can be dusty. This will affect their ability for bug-trapping.

17. After vacuuming, pick up all stray animals which may have crawled or fallen off your box spring and mattress.

18. If you want to keep your clean clothing safe from bed bugs, you can store it in Ziploc bags, contractor bags, or storage bins. For your clean clothing to be safe from bedbugs, store it in an airtight contractor bag or resealable bags (such as Ziploc) or bins. ASG dust does not need to be used for clothing storage.

All participants should complete Steps 19-25.

19. Place pillow covers on your new pillows.

20. Lay clean white bed linens out on the bedding. The clean linens make it easier to

spot bed bugs and blood stains, if they are still present, after you've treated the area.

21. Check the sheets every day for bugs, molted skins, blood spots and stains that look like black ink. Check your bed sheets each day to look for insects, molted hides, blood stains, and black spots. Bed bugs can still be present in the home even after you've protected it. The information can be useful, especially for those who do not react when bitten. The bugs may still be in your bed if the bed is isolated.

22. To ensure that bed bugs do not live in your bed, repeat the vacuuming and cleaning steps described above. Repeat all treatment approximately every two-weeks until there are no more signs of bedbug bites or evidence.

23. Use caution to prevent spreading bed bugs or eggs collected by the vacuum to your home. Learn more in Chapter 11 about

vacuuming properly and how to handle your vacuum.

24. Review your preventive measures daily. Maintain the containment area. Make sure you inspect your encasements to check for holes and tears.

25. Avoid allowing pets near the infested area.

Please consider the following:

Wooden Bedframes. If you own a wooden frame, disassemble the bed frame completely and wash it thoroughly with Murphy’s Oil Soap. Murphy's Oil is sprayed onto all bedframe elements (not a rag). Take care to inspect all cracks in wood, as well as joints. Murphy's Oil Soap can kill bed bugs immediately, but provides no lasting protection. Once the oil has dried, spread a thin film of silica on top.

Upholstered Headboards & Footboards - Any type of upholstery can be very challenging to remove. The upholstered headboards or footboards can be taken off the frames to treat. Use ASG Dust and a vacuum.

Do I have to throw out my mattress?

The question is understandable. You should keep your bed for many reasons.

First of all, bedbug infestations don't just occur on the bed. Your problem won't be resolved by throwing your mattress or box spring away. The infestation will return quickly if you buy a new mattress.

In the second place, if you do not handle the mattress properly during removal, it is possible that the bed bug and its eggs will be scattered throughout your house.

You should consider also where the mattress will go when you dispose of it. What will happen to it? Are there any chances that it will be accidentally touched by others? Although it might seem like a great idea to get rid of the bed, you will only spread the problem to the rest of the neighborhood.

Bed bugs can be a real problem, but throwing out the mattress is not going to solve it.

Though you have a strong reason to get rid of your bedding, mattress and box spring, it is still possible that there will be other reasons. To do this properly, take the necessary precautions. It is possible to remove the majority of infestations at once if you have a bed that needs replacement. The answer is no. As much effort as is needed to protect and treat your bed, it will also take time and energy to get rid of your box spring and mattress. It might bring you peace of mind, especially when you are dealing with an infestation.

Follow these steps to keep yourself and your neighbors safe.

You should carefully wrap any items you intend to discard in plastic, shrink-wrap or bubble wrap. You can use duct tap to stop the wrap from coming apart.

* Handle infected items with extreme caution. Don't drop them or shake them.

Mark all infested objects with a red spray-paint to alert others.

* Coordinate your disposal schedule of infested objects with the trash collection day for your area. These items should not be left outside for long.

It is important to remember that the bedbug population will not only be contained in your discarded items. A new mattress can become infested very quickly. You should protect your newly purchased bed with encasements that cover both the mattress and the spring. The only way to be sure that they will not spread bed bugs into an infested area is to protect them with the proper bed bug cover. Encasements may not be completely impervious to bed bug infestations, however they can only access their outer surface. It is important to make sure that the bed encasement doesn't get damaged during its delivery or installation.

Vacuuming Instructions - Chapter 11

Vacuuming the bed or other areas where bed bugs are present is an effective method to quickly reduce their numbers. You should not use vacuuming as your sole weapon to fight bedbugs.

The majority of vacuum cleaners work well for this type of treatment. I find that the ones with hoses, bags, and attachments to make cleanup easier are most useful. But many have had success with canisters. Be sure to choose a vacuum that has a HEPA filter system.

Vacuum Cleaners and Attachments to Avoid:

Some battery-charged vacuum cleaners or portable models don't provide enough suction to eliminate bed bugs, their eggs and other pests.

It is to the benefit of bugs, not you, to use brush hose accessories with bristles. Such surfaces tend to attract bed bugs and their egg. Scrub surfaces with a scrubber that is thrown away.

The Best Way to Use a Vacuum when You Are Trying to Remove Bed Bugs

It is important to handle the vacuum carefully when removing bed bugs. The vacuum can be infected. Use a cleaner separate from that which you regularly use. However, it isn't always possible or practical to do so. Below are steps you can take to decrease the chances that bed bugs will be found in your vacuum.

1. Dust a small amount ASG in the bag of your vacuum or into the canister to start

eliminating bed bugs. This helps to make conditions more conducive for the vermin.

2. Seal the vacuum into a contractor's plastic bag when you finish vacuuming.

3. Empty the contents of your vacuum bag, or the canister once you’ve taken it outside. Place the bag in another bag for contractors. Then, place the sealed bag in a container with a secure lid.

4. Use a canister to vacuum. The canister should be thoroughly cleaned, as should the filter.

5. If you want to get rid of bed bugs, steam can be sprayed on the underside of the vacuum near the rotating bristles.

6. Once you've finished vacuuming the entire vacuum system, dust a few more ASG particles into the vacuum bags, canisters, and all other vacuum parts which may have been in contact with bed bugs.

7. You can seal your vacuum cleaner in an airtight container with Nuvan (r) ProStrip. This product releases an invisible vapor of pesticide from the strip. This is fatal to all forms of bed bugs including eggs. Nuvan ProStrips are covered in the next chapter. ProStrips are only effective for 7-10 business days, which means you'll be without your vacuum cleaner if you select this option.

Vacuuming Techniques

* If you can, use a light or UV source. These UV flashlights cost little and will be useful for the whole bed bug removal process.

The magnifying lens is useful because bedbugs can be found almost anywhere. As small as the crevice at the top of a screw, bedbugs can be found.

• Move the nozzle slowly over infested surfaces.

You can use the nozzle's tip, a scraper that you throw away or a brush to remove the eggs.

The vacuuming technique should be applied to all other materials, including carpets, upholstery, or any furniture. More items vacuumed, more bedbugs you'll remove.

It is common for bed bugs to congregate and hide along the edges of carpets where silica dust has been applied as a containment. Although you will likely want to vacuum up these areas, maintaining the integrity of containment is crucial. To maintain the integrity of the containment, I vacuum two or three foot sections at a given time. I then apply the dust again to ensure that the barrier is maintained before I continue to the following section. The importance of this is especially high when you have heavy infestations.

Remember how early in the book, I cautioned you to not vacuum up bugs before following the rest of the instructions? As I described it, doing things the right way is hard work. But if, after vacuuming your carpet, you apply ASG dust, the bugs will disperse all over. Avoid this situation at any cost.

You will never be successful in eliminating the infestation by using just one type of treatment. You should remain vigilant, even though you may be relieved to have physically removed so many bugs. Now that you have the upper-hand, don't give up.

Chapter 13: Steam Instructions

Steam treatment for bedbugs is an alternative method that's used by most pest control experts. If done right and with proper equipment, steam instantly kills any stage of the bed bug's life cycle. Use steam only after you have vacuumed, and not before ASG dust. This will most likely negate any killing power of ASG.

You should avoid steaming the edges. Even though bugs tend to love hiding in carpet edges, vacuuming them instead of steaming is the best option. Reapplying the ASG Dust immediately afterward will also help. Because it's so crucial to maintain the integrity the room containment, (see chapter 7), in order to stop the bugs moving to other parts of your residence. The room containment should be set up before any other treatments are carried out and maintained through the entire treatment phase to prevent an infestation spreading.

See "Vacuuming" Techniques in Chapter 11 for a reminder on the best way to vacuum around carpet edges.

A Few Tips on Steam

Steam is dangerous. Keep your focus and follow the manufacturer's directions.

* Use only dry vapor steam units to avoid mold. In the event that you use a regular steamer, it will cause excess moisture to be left in whatever surface is being treated.

The steam can clean up almost everything in your home, from furniture to baseboards.

Please do not apply steam directly to wires and electrical outlets.

Please avoid steaming your carpet's edges.

Bed bugs must be killed by steam, not blowing them off.

Bed bugs are attracted to heat. According to the manufacturers, the temperature on the tip of the steamed should be at 200 degrees Fahrenheit. It will steam surfaces to about 155-165 F, which instantly kills bed bugs. My recommendations for a good steamer are in my Bed Bug Supply Manual.

Important Things to Consider When Buying a Steamer

The steam must be dry or "dry vapour" (this is crucial).

According to the manufacturer, the heat at the tip should be at least 200F.

• Larger water chamber for fewer starts and stops during the steaming procedure

This cord can be used as an extension cord.

• A boiler with a good warranty

Steamers can be used to kill bugs, but many aren't. Vapamore MR-100 steamer is what I use, it is affordable dry vapor steamer and also meets all criteria listed above. It retails at around $300 to $350. Bed Bug Supply

Manual contains more information and tells you where to purchase it.

Also, you could call local businesses to find out if they rent steamers. My nearest steamer rental was located about 40 minutes away. So I bought my steamer. For a rental, expect to pay between $50 and 100 dollars for a two or three-day period.

The Application of Steam

Be extremely careful when you use a steamer. Its high temperatures could cause serious burns. You should move very slowly to ensure that bed bugs or eggs are all killed by the steam. If you use the correct temperatures, it is possible to expect about 1 inch of movement per second. Install a thin fabric over the nozzle of the steamer if it is coming out at a rapid pace. You can reduce the strength of the steam by putting a thin cloth over the nozzle.

Amorphous Silica Gel Dust - Chapter 13

In earlier chapters we've already discussed the 100% amorphous amorphous gel desiccant. This dust is also called ASG and CimeXa. You will learn more about this material in this chapter.

What We Already Understand

I think that bed bug killing is best done with 100% Amorphous Silica Gel Dust.

The dust may be called "desiccant", "CimeXa", "ASG" or even "silica".

This product is a bed bug repellent.

ASG dust is able to absorb a protective coating that keeps moisture within the bed bug's body. This kills them in 24 to 48 hours.

* The material’s static cling provides more exposure to the environment than most other materials, and this leads to faster death compared with any other substance.

Chapter 14: Organization Of The Belongings, Their Containment And Treatment

Next comes the somewhat long and tedious job of sorting personal items and placing them in bags or containers. Although this step will require some effort, it is crucial.

It is important that you do not let up, even though you've come a long way. The importance of continuing to move forward is greater than ever. Your previous efforts won't be worth anything if you stop now.

As you go through this step, mark each bag/container with what's inside and whether the items are "possibly safe" or infested. The treatment methods used will depend on how each bag is labelled, so try to keep like-items together.

Step 1. Sort and organize washables, including clothes, curtains, shoes, bedding, stuffed animals, pillows,etc. This includes washing the items with hot water. Dry them at maximum heat. It is important to use heat. Therefore, if your clothes are clean you do not need to rewash them. You can put your clothes into the dryer at high heat for about 30 minutes. Not everything can be put through the washer or dryer.

Step 2: Bag and organize hard items like electronics, books or paintings. Also, treat delicate items and items that cannot be washed. The items are more difficult to handle. ASG dust may be used on some of the items, but you should use discretion. Ziploc and contractor bags can be used to seal these bags. If you want to eliminate bed bugs in the bag, there are a couple of options.

There are two options available to you:

1. The bed bugs will die if they are not fed. As bed bugs can survive up to 18 months without eating, you will need to keep your item locked away.

2. Nuvan ProStrips should be placed inside the bag with items. Seal the bag. Be careful to not overstuff them. ProStrips seem more effective if you leave some airspace in between. You should also make sure to check that the bag seals tightly and carefully follow all manufacturer instructions.

All bed bug life cycles, eggs included, are killed by the pesticide released from ProStrips. You should seal the items and leave them in their bags sealed for at least one week up to 10 days. ProStrips takes longer to destroy the bed bug eggs than the bed bug hatchlings, while younger bed bugs die faster than the adult bed bugs.

3. For smaller appliances in the home, portable heaters can be purchased. They are more expensive but extremely efficient. They cost anywhere from $200 up to $350, depending on their size. These portable heaters can be found in different sizes. They can be very helpful for items like books, electronic devices, documents, etc. that are

harder to treat. They can be used to heat luggage that has been returned from traveling to make sure bed bugs do not enter your home. Bed Bug Supply Manual contains more information on portable heaters for bed bugs.

4. If you choose this method, add dry ice to the bags before vacuum sealing them. Bed bugs need oxygen to survive. Dry ice can be added to bags prior to vacuum sealing them if this is the method you prefer. To small bags with smaller items (such as framed art or purses), add 1 pound of dried ice. Two pounds of dried ice can be added to bags of medium size containing suitcases and small appliances. Three pounds is needed for bags of large size containing furniture, entertainment systems and other items. The dry ice's carbon dioxide will remove any oxygen from the bag. You can do this in about 48-hours, but it is better to double the time.

5. It is possible to run some non-delicate toys in a mesh bag through a dishwashing machine with the "heated drying" option turned on. The only time I recommend this is when you know for sure that you have an infestation in your home. Otherwise, you could be putting yourself at risk by moving items infested to an infected area. Be very careful if you decide to choose this option. Avoid it, unless you have no other choice.

In Step 3, you should protect all treated items by storing them in new bins or contractor bags. This will prevent the bed bugs from coming back.

Step 4: Get rid of any smaller items that are no longer needed. However, only throw them away if the items fit into an contractor's bag or a Ziploc bag. The item does not have to be large enough to fit into a contractor bag or a Ziploc bag.

When you're considering tossing larger objects, like dressers, nightstands, or any other item that can't be sealed safely inside a contractor-bag, plastic bag, etc., keep in mind what you already read regarding the dangers associated with throwing a mattress that is infested away. Same rules are applicable to these larger items. This makes it much simpler and safer to deal with these kinds of items.

Bags should be sealed tightly with a tight seal. You can either mark the bag with "bedbugs", or you can keep it in a safe place where others will not touch the bags until garbage day.

Let's Roll!

By this point, all clutter infested spaces should have been removed. You should have no clothing in your room or closet, and no picture on the wall. Also, there shouldn't any throw rugs or clutter on the ground. The bugs have been placed where they want to be because you followed every step and maintained the integrity in your room. Are you ready to go? Let's go!

Chapt. 15: Time to kill some bedbugs!

The moment has finally arrived. Your preparations have taken a lot of time. It's time to get rid of some bugs.

This is what you'll need

* ASG dust

* A pest-control duster.

Paintbrushes or cosmetic brushes with extremely fine bristles are ideal for applying paint to areas where more precision is required.

It is possible to use a screwdriver for loosening electrical outlets and switch plates.

Dust mask

* Vacuum cleaners with HEPA filters

Instructions

1. ASG can be applied lightly to all surfaces, including carpets and floors.

This stuff will remain on your floor or carpets for a few months. If you vacuum, you can do so as many times as you wish. When you finish cleaning the carpet or floor, reapply ASG.

2. Take everything apart and pull furniture away from the wall. The furniture needs to be flipped over so that all the areas can be treated. Also, drawers should be removed. The contents of drawers must have been removed by this point. However, if not, put everything left inside into sealed bags, or other containers that are resistant to bed bugs.

3. Bed bugs may be present on couches, loveseats or chairs with upholstered covers. They should all be treated as you would treat your bed. If you suspect bed bugs, remove the cushions from your furniture

and clean every crevice and crack possible. Do not dust surfaces where people sit. This is where attention to details are required. Apply paint with a duster and brush to zippers. Cover the seams. You can continue to use the furniture like you normally do. Your furniture will now be a bed bug killing station, with you as the bait. (Sorry!) It's almost the end of your battle against bed bugs!

4. If you want to isolate a furniture piece after it has been treated for bed bugs, then place interceptors that allow the crawlers to climb under its legs. Bed Bug Supply Manual contains more details about bedbug interceptors.

5. Release the switch plates and electrical outlet covers. Bugs love to nestle inside these. ASG powder can be used to dust the inside, but a pest control duster is preferred. Once you have tightened them, apply ASG.

6. ASG dust can be applied in all cracks, crevices or voids. Be sure to also dust around appliances and stationary items. ASG Dust will last for 10 years without being disturbed. Therefore, it is recommended that you apply a thin, even coating in all the non-traffic areas around your home. This includes behind cabinet doors, within wall voids, and on door frames if caulk has not been used. ASG will protect your home from other pests as well, such as silverfish, ants and cockroaches.

7. Caulking and sealing voids, cracks or crevices isn't recommended until all of them have been treated properly with ASG powder. It's okay if bedbugs can get into these places at this time, as we want them to come into contact first with ASG. A crack, crevice or void would be the only exception. It allows bugs access to other areas of your house without being obstructed. In this case, seal the crack or crevice immediately after spraying ASG powder. Later we'll

discuss the caulking, sealing and other methods.

8. While some people consider the next step optional, I like to perform it on every infestation. You should check first with your renter if you live in a rental.

Use a studfinder and mark out the pattern of holes you'll drill in walls between the beams. They should just be big enough for your duster tip to fit into.

o Try to drill at an angle of 45° at the spot where the baseboard's top meets the walls. If you do this, instead of painting and spackling the holes, it will be easier to use caulk.

ASG dust can be applied into the wall gap at different locations.

This will reduce bed bug survival rates and protect your house from infestations in the future. In apartment buildings, condos townhomes and duplexes this is particularly important. The next step is to paint and patch the holes.

9. Apply ASG dust in a thin coat to the other surfaces.

10. If you notice live bed bugs, eggs or castings on a surface, then use ASG dust or ASG steamer depending on its size.

11. Monitor bed bugs activity and maintain integrity in the contained areas.

Pesticides alone won't kill bed bugs.

No pesticides needed to get rid of bed bugs. ASG dust was found to be more efficient than other poisons at killing bed bugs in scientific studies. In my experience, I've never had to apply pesticides in order to rid myself of a bedbug problem.

Chapter 15: Pest-Proofing Rooms

How can you make your house resistant to bedbugs? To a certain extent, yes.

This will require a bit of effort, but it can be done. That's why many overlook this method. But this is not a time to be lax. If you successfully complete this step, then you have made a significant progress in the fight against bedbugs.

Your home has come a very long way from the first time you noticed that there was a bedbug problem. The job is now complete.

This is what you'll need

* Caulk gun

This latex paintable caulk is a great alternative to traditional silicone.

* Joint compound

Filler for wood (if necessary)

* Expanding Foam (if necessary)

• Utility knife

You can also use paper towels.

It is important to ensure that bedbugs cannot move from room to room. In order to minimize the bed bug population, you should also remove any cracks, crevices, or voids that may exist in your room. It is a good rule to follow that bed bugs will be present in any crevice large enough for the edge or a credit cards. The second rule is to seal all visible crevices.

Cracks and crevices can be found in:

* Furniture

You can find headboards and bedframes in the following categories:

Trim work

Molding

* Frames for doors and windows

Pictures

Drywall

Any other things you may see

It should be clear to you by now which areas are problematic for the elimination and control of bed bugs. You can use these suggestions and combine them with your creative ideas to design the perfect bed bug proofing solution for your home.

Bed Bug-Proofing Tips

ASG dust should be lightly applied to any cracks or crevices that you intend to seal. Paintable latex sealant, woodfiller, expanding foam or paint can be used to seal any cracks.

A bunch of paper towels is needed, as you can clean excess caulk with a wet paper towel.

A handy tool can give your caulking a smoother finish.

These are a few tips for those who have never used caulk before:

If you want to get more caulk out of your tube, cut it at an angled angle. You can cut further into the tube to get more caulk.

It is also necessary to poke a hole in the inner tube. The seal is located approximately three inches beneath the surface that will need to be punctured. This pin can be found on most caulkguns.

It is only necessary to apply a very small amount at one time for cracks. It is important to remember that the tip can be cut off but it cannot be added back. Starting with smaller cracks and crevices you can work your way upwards to larger ones, while removing the most of the caulk tip.

If you want to seal a crevice, hold your gun with the proper angle.

* Push the trigger to release the caulk from the tube. Moving the tip slowly along the

crevice is the best way to achieve a good seal. You can spread the caulk using your finger to seal crevices. Once you start, the process will become second nature.

There will always be messes. But they are easy to clean with a paper or damp cloth.

Latex caulk can only be used to seal smaller gaps. If the gap is larger, you may need expanding foam to fill it or an alternative repair.

Chapter 16: Monitor & Maintain

Congratulations! It's over.

But don't lose your guard. You must maintain the ASG Dust and watch for bedbug signs to avoid a resurgence.

Regular inspections will be your best tool for monitoring. Inspect the infested parts of your home using the same methods you used during your initial inspection. If you discover any living bed bugs, or even eggs, make sure to vacuum or steam them. You should immediately apply ASG dust in any areas where you vacuum or clean.

It is important to clean any infested areas regularly. It is important to clean bedbugs because they are such nasty creatures. After cleaning everything, I may use Lysol and Murphy's Oil to clean. I then dust with ASG after finishing.

It is important to remember that the mere presence or absence of bedbug bites does not mean bed bugs have been found. Some people don't have any kind of skin reaction from bed bug bites.

Passive Monitoring Systems

It is also possible to monitor with climb-up interceptors. You only need to make sure the mattress or any other piece of furniture has been pulled away from a wall, and that no blankets touch the floor. It should only be possible for bedbugs to get into the bed via the bed posts. Remember that bed bugs interceptors are designed to isolate the mattress.

Also, you can use bed bug traps that rely on CO2 or heat. Buy ready-made bed bug traps, or create your own. The homemade device can work as well or better than the commercially available traps because it produces more CO2. In the Bed Bug Supply Manual, I will describe this process.

Your Most Important Monitoring Tool

In the end though, you will prove to be your most useful monitoring tool. It will make it easier to monitor if you do regular inspections, continue sleeping on "protected bed" sheets with a cotton white blanket and remain in the same white sheeting.

Ch. 18. Conclusion

There you go!

The world is divided into two distinct camps: those with experience dealing with bed bugs and others who have not.

Although it is difficult, bed bug infestations can be managed. It is commendable that you took the steps you did to deal with your infestation. Bed bugs are a difficult enemy to defeat. Only education and prevention can help us win. Probabilities are that someone close to you has also dealt with an outbreak at one point or another in their life. Now you can help.

The best is my wish for you.

The Most Frequently Asked Question

Why did I contract bedbugs?

The source of bed bugs can be difficult to determine. Movie theaters are a common source, as well as planes, trains, buses, hotels and friends. You can get them from other apartments or condominiums. It is possible that bedbugs could come from anywhere.

Are bed bugs dangerous?

There is no evidence that bedbugs transmit disease. It is only secondary infection that can result from scratching or neglecting bed bugs' bites. Secondary infections can occur from scratching bed bug bites. You should resist the temptation to scratch and instead treat bites as you would mosquito bites. In terms of emotional impact, bedbugs can be very damaging. People who have bed bug infestations often experience severe stress, anxiety and lack of sleep.

Where can I travel without being infected by bed bugs?

Travelers should be informed about bedbugs. Always inspect your hotel room before settling into it. For your inspection, pack a light (even if you can get the LED-keychain variety). Also bring some gloves. This inspection will be centered around the beds. When you're alone in a hotel room, you can request that someone help you lift items to inspect them. Start by lifting the headboard. This is normally held to the wall using brackets. To access the rear, first lift the headboard up a couple of inches. After pulling back the bed sheets, check for blood spots. Check for piping around the mattress and boxspring. Check under and inside the drawers in your bedside table. Then, if everything is clear in all of these locations, you can relax and enjoy your evening. Look for spots in your sheets the next day. They defecate immediately after eating.

You may find old bed bug evidence. This does not necessarily indicate that the hotel's cleanliness is poor. The front desk should be informed discreetly of what you discovered. Request a different room, one that is not adjacent to the room just vacated. Hospitality industry's public relations problems are caused by bedbugs. By avoiding a competitor who is just as likely also to have bedbugs, the hospitality industry may be less willing to discuss this problem. Communication is crucial. Hotel and motel staff should take pride in their bed bug prevention programs, and they should show guests how to do an inspection to make sure that everyone is bed bug free.

You should avoid unpacking your bags into drawers. Instead, keep them closed in a luggage stand that has been pulled out from the wall. Never leave luggage on a mattress.

What can I expect if I've just come back from an environment where bed bugs may be present?

You should wash your clothes as soon as you bring them home. In the event that you discover bedbugs in your hotel room after moving in, you can ask for them to cover all laundry costs and even steam-clean your luggage. Asking is worth it, even if the hotel refuses. If you're going to unpack at home, you need to do it on a surface that allows you see the bed bugs. Don't use carpet! To take clothes to the wash, unpack into bags made of plastic. It is important to inspect and vacuum your suitcases, or freeze them in the case of extreme cold.

Do bed bugs spread on the body?

A bed bug could travel to you, or on the clothing you wear. The bed bug cannot hide well if you move around a lot. Most likely, bedbugs are spread by luggage, suitcases, backpacks, laptops, mattresses and old furniture.

What can I do to my pets when I've got bed bugs?

There is a widespread belief that bedbugs only feed upon humans. They prefer human hosts. Others who work in pest control have said that bed bugs have been seen feeding on dogs. While they won't settle on your pet the way fleas will, pets can still carry and harbor bed bugs. Your pet should have the same sleeping place as you.

How long do bedbugs take to eliminate?

You can determine how long it will take you to rid yourself of bed bugs by considering a few factors. These include how long you have had the bugs in the house, what you do to combat them, how well you treat the infestation, whether the people who live in the home are cooperating with your efforts, or if the treatment you used was ineffective. The following information will give you more details about the factors that influence how long it takes to get rid of bed bugs:

What is the duration of bed bug activity? The bugs will be in the bed, if they are new. It's possible to find a single bug in your bed if lucky. It is important to check all areas of the room, and to apply one single treatment to eradicate bedbugs.

You must have acted quickly after you found the infestation. Don't wait for long or you will give the vermin time to reproduce. However, ineffective measures will only worsen the situation. The majority of insecticides sprays do not work to kill bed bug eggs, while an insecticide explosion will only spread the pests further into your house.

What are the extent and severity of the problems? Infestations that have not been treated for a while may be characterized by a high number of bed bugs, or insects.

There is how much mess? There are many places for bugs to hide when there's a lot clutter.

Which type of bed is present in this area and where is it located?

* What's the environmental condition of the infestation? Since bedbugs can be spread between dwellings in an apartment, condo, townhome, or duplex, these situations are more complex.

In my opinion, it would take between two and three treatment sessions properly carried out over a period of about three to five days to eradicate bed bugs. But you'll be able cut down the infestation to at least 85 percent within 24 to 72 hours. The first time they treated their bed bugs, many people have never seen a single one again. It may take you longer to treat your infestation because every case is unique.

Why not use pesticides rather?

It is my belief that only a pest management specialist should use toxic pesticides to exterminate bed bugs. By applying harmful substances, you could make your infestation worse. It can even put your family at risk. ASG Dust is also more effective at killing bedbugs than pesticides, according to recent research. When you use pesticides, it is important to read the labels and make sure that they are followed.

What should I do if i am a tenant or a homeowner?

It is important that tenants do not treat any bedbug infestations until their landlord or the building manager has confirmed it. Responding quickly is the responsibility of landlords and property managers. In the event that your property manager doesn't respond to your concerns, you may need to contact your city's construction department. The residents and the landlords should work together to eradicate bed bugs.

What should I do if bed bugs are present in my home?

While your residence may be infested, moving is not recommended. Take care not to bring bedbugs along with your move if circumstances require it.

Follow all steps outlined in the guide prior to moving. The steps include vacuuming the mattress, applying ASG powder as instructed, organizing your items, and cleaning. It is important to kill bed bugs in your clothing and other personal belongings. If you are leaving an infested home, there is no way to make any cuts.

If I want to do the job myself but hire someone else, is that a problem?

The chances are that you read this book because you want to eradicate bed bugs in whatever way possible. After reading my account of bed bug infestation, I can assure you that hiring pest control professionals does not ensure better results. Some people may feel more confident with an experienced technician's guidance. I will encourage you, in the end to go with your instincts and choose what's best for you. It is only you who can get rid of bed bugs in your house. It is possible to relieve the burden of bed bugs if a professional can be trusted and who has the necessary experience.

When you have the money to hire an expert, you need to be able to pick out the best one. It is likely that there are both bad and good companies operating in your region. To determine the best companies to eliminate bed bugs, you need to know which ones have had a successful history. You should also consider the company's price and perform some homework.

Pricing:

For accurate comparisons, you should ask the companies how much each technician will charge per hour. If a company uses two technicians, you can make a fair comparison by asking how much each technician costs.

Most likely, the price is too high because this company doesn't care about treating bed bugs. You can get them to do the work if you're willing to pay a fortune, but they want it avoided at all costs.

The price of the job should not be too low. This is indicative of inexperience. If a company has experience with bed bugs, it will not price the work low.

Do your homework:

Review the online reviews by visiting sites like Angie's List or Yelp.

Check the Better Business Bureau for any complaints that have been lodged against the company.

If the company is unable to offer references, ask for a list of previous clients.

ASK how much is covered by their liability insurance. Do not call if the company does not carry liability insurance.

If so, what is included? Which guarantees are offered? The majority of companies don't guarantee apartments or units with multiple families due to the high risk of reinfestation. You can still ask the company to guarantee a home if it's occupied by occupants of multifamily or apartment dwellings. The level of assurance they have in their treatments will be reflected by the strength of their guarantee.

* Find out if the company offers a treatment for cracks and crevices. Bed bugs can hide in these crevices, and it's important to make sure the company you choose has a strategy for tackling them.

How many treatments is included in the price? Two or three treatments may be needed, if you ask an experienced firm. Two weeks should pass between treatments, with each taking at least two-and-a half hours.

Do not let the company rely solely on pesticides. It is important to use non-chemical techniques in order to eliminate bedbugs permanently.

* Determine if a company has bed bug experts on its staff. The most experienced companies usually employ dedicated teams to treat bed bug outbreaks. If the company does have dedicated teams to treat bed bug outbreaks, it's a sign that they are experienced.

Chapter 17: Bed Bugs Basics

Appearance, Biology and Fitness

Identifying the bed bug can be tricky, since ticks and other insects are mistakenly regarded as bed bugs. This is especially true when you see them in your home. The texture, size, and shape of an unwanted bug, as well as its behavior, can help you identify it before you try to get rid of it.

Insects the size and shape of a grain or rice feed off blood. Cimex Lectularius belongs to the Cimicidae. This rusty red, non-winged, nocturnal creature has 6 legs and 2 antennae. It is active only at night. These insects are often found in wooden frames, furniture and luggage. They can also be seen hiding inside wall cracks or crevices. In the night, bedbugs feed on people and pets that are sleeping.

A quarter of an inch is the size of adult bed bugs. Their flat body, with an oval shape and their squat heads can easily be identified by sight. A bed bug's body puffs up when they finish feeding. They also have a vibrant, temporary red colour.

Male bed bugs, on the other hand, have hardened external male genitalia. This unique "traumatic" process allows for mating. The genders of both inflated animals after blood meals are unusually similar.

During her life, a female bed bug may have 500 or more offspring. In a short time, these tiny rust-colored pests could turn into an enormous infestation. They lay up to 50 1mm eggs per cluster in places where they don't feed, such as cracks or mattress seams. Within one to two months, these eggs develop into 2 - 5 mm long nymphs.

They are the exact same size as adults but have a different color. In the nymph stage, they change color from an off white to a yellowish translucent hue. After shedding their skin five times (each time needing a meal of blood), they turn mahogany and develop into an adult measuring 7 mm. This takes less than 3 weeks (unless it is colder). They can also be identified during the daylight hours by their rusty markings left on bedding and mattresses. Adults may live for ten months or even a whole year. Three to four offspring are produced.

A bedbug's feeding mechanism is quite fascinating. Bed bugs are drawn to carbon dioxide from the hosts, and feed off the warm-blooded blood. This includes humans and pets. The feeding organ (proboscis) is used to penetrate prey skin. The mammal is then injected with saliva, which helps to keep the blood from clotting. Some people may experience itching, and even allergic reactions, as a result.

In just 3 to 10 minute, these tiny cockroaches can drink as much blood as they do in a human. It is estimated that they eat between 8 and 10 times a week, although adults can go up to 14 days without eating.

Bed Bugs History

Cimex Lecturlarius is a descendant of the Mediterranean, where human beings first began to inhabit caves. Bugs have always lived in caves inhabited by humans, and they've been eating bats. Cimex (meaning bug) was used in the Roman Empire, while Lecturlarius (referring to a sleeping or resting area) is also used.

The first time the term "bugge" (originally spelled as bug) was heard, it was in 1620s. In the later years, the word was also used for ladybugs or insects of similar size. Sources have consistently used bed bug as the name of the pest, even though it is often hyphenated with bed-bug. Also called mahogany louse.

In the past, their impact on human society was far less severe. Egyptians boiled bugs to make potions for diseases. Some Egyptians drank them as a remedy to snakebites.

Bed bug remedies were used in Europe as well as in North America in the early 1900s. These bloodsucking bugs were believed to have been used in ancient Greece to treat bites or cure ear problems. Guettard suggested using them in the 1800s to treat hysteria.

The human race flourished. As a result, insects multiplied in villages and towns throughout Asia and Europe. The Northern Hemisphere is home to a wide range of bugs that thrive under temperate conditions.

Germany and France both witnessed the development of the bed bugs in their heated sleeping areas and around fires for cooking. In 1666, fir logs used in rebuilding London were found to contain bugs. These first appeared on newly built homes in England. England also reported the first bugs to be found in the country back in

1538. From there, the bug was carried to America by European settlers and flourished over the next few decades.

After the 18th century, North America was plagued by infestations. For the purpose of killing bugs, crevices and cracked were often soaked in boiling boiled water. Sassafras was used to make beds. It was believed by many that dirty places were more susceptible to infestation. The most common attack sites were dusty, dirty hotels and trains.

In order to rid their homes of the unwanted pests, the wealthy began undertaking extensive housekeeping. Bugs were wiped out by frequent cleaning, dusting and dusting in wall cracks, upholstery and crevices. One third of the homes in America by early 20th Century were infested. The low income area (possibly unhygienic) and areas with poor preservation had been impacted.

Planning and implementing extermination programs was much easier than executing them. In hotels and other wealthy places, the bugs would hide in clothes and suitcases seams.

In time, as new methods of pest control with residual pesticides like DDT (and Malathion), were implemented and washing machines became more commonplace, their chances of surviving diminished. Bed bugs were eradicated by pest controllers in 1950, but recurred again during the 1990s. The bugs spread from high-incidence areas to low or negligible incidence areas, such as airports, hotel rooms, and cargo room. A shift in focus was made from public campaigns to pest prevention programs.

Bites and Symptoms

In order to facilitate blood sucking, the well-developed head proboscis of bed bugs pierces human skin. At first glance, you will see a rash around the bite area. These rashes are caused by an allergic reaction that is itchy and irritable. Even though the bite itself is painless, a small, red wheal appears, and then slowly becomes a spot of red.

It is called cimicosis. These bites will follow an exact pattern on your skin. While some bites are not visible on the skin, others will cause an obvious rash. The bites can:

Blisters

* Welts

* Localized swelling

Large red wheals

* A reddish skin tone

Blood

* Scratching infection

This can lead to a loss of skin tissues.

Infection with harmful pathogens may occur in bed bugs, since they feed on both animals and humans. The tiny insect is not likely to transmit any diseases. Bug bites do not usually cause serious injury, but itching can lead to nasty scars and discomfort. If you scratch your skin repeatedly, it can cause it to break out and expose the skin to infections.

During the night, bug bites may be seen on the forearms, hands, backs, necks, legs and any other exposed area. It doesn't matter where the bug feeds, so long as he gets a regular flow of blood. Many people don't notice that they are being bitten while they sleep until they start to see blisters. Bug bites can be mistaken for mosquito bites. Some people may feel nothing at all, while others will develop welts.

Chapter 18: What To Do About Bites And Rashes?

In reality, the battle continues against these quarter-inch pests who feed off of our blood. They do this while we snore in the dark. The unpleasant experience of waking up to huge wheals or red patches and itchy, dry skin can be a nightmare. Inflammations and rashes should be treated promptly to avoid infection and serious breakouts.

Sometimes a rash will appear days or hours after an insect bite. If you have an intense allergy to insect bites, the rashes can be so severe that they last up to a week and become welts. The risk is that a secondary skin disease will develop, causing more severe problems than a mere bug bite.

Treatment

When left unattended, rashes or swellings can be very persistent and leave scars on the skin. Certain medical and herbal remedies can ease discomfort from rashes.

Many medications can relieve itchy blisters, but let's try some home remedies.

Homemade remedies

As an example of symptom relief, the first step is to wash off infected skin with lukewarm tepid water. It is important to use soap to clean any bites and to avoid touching the area too much. Resist the urge to scratch, regardless of how itchy it may be. If you have a lot of bacteria on your hands, they can cause an infection and irritate a blister. A simple baking soda-water mixture can help to relieve itching and pain. After a few minutes, or depending on severity of rash, peel off the mixture with cold, clean water.

Water and aspirin can be used to treat swollen, irritated skin. To reduce the swelling, crush an aspirin into a powder and combine it with some water. This can be accomplished by making a paste from powdered oats.

One way to quickly clear the bite rash is by using a cotton wool ball dipped in Alka-Seltzer. In addition, you can try using Witch Hazel and lemon juice.

Topical Creams or Oral Antihistamines

You don't have to resort to homemade solutions if you can find a topical cream or antihistamine that works. After washing off the rash, apply the cream liberally to the affected skin every 6 to 12 hours.

It is important to take oral antihistamines in order to reduce the severity and duration of rashes. Bredanyl can help relieve itchy, rashes by reducing the severity of the rash. Never let bedbugs bite again. You should clean and change the sheets of your bed after an episode with bed bugs.

Zyrtec® and Claritin® are two antihistamines which do not cause sleepiness, don’t require prescriptions and can be purchased at any local pharmacy. Prednisone oral steroids (available on prescription) can also be used to treat itches caused by trails of bug bites.

Topical creams provide relief by eliminating the itching. Itching creams like cortisone or steroid can help to reduce the itch and even blisters. Calamine lotions can protect your skin and help it heal, which will prevent rashes. Calamine lotions also dry up the rash quicker, speeding the healing process.

Ibuprofen or naproxen will reduce the inflammation of your skin. Anesthetics that contain pramoxine or creams containing dephendrydramine may also help to reduce pain.

Seeking a doctor for health care

When lower dose creams fail to have an effect, and the skin rash continues, you may need a prescription. You can get help from your doctor if you're not sure what caused the skin reaction. The rash is unlikely to be caused by bed bugs, as they tend hide during the daylight hours.

There is a risk that you will develop a skin infection, especially if the blisters are scratched. You should consult your doctor as soon as you see the rash becoming a lesion or severe welt.

He may also prescribe antibiotic ointments and oral antibiotics in the event of a severe bacterial infection. Corticosteroids (or Epinephrine) injections may be needed in extremely rare allergic conditions that involve the entire organism.

What to do before you visit your health care physician

Be sure to prepare an organized chronological case before seeing your doctor. Your doctor will need to know your exact location. Before seeking medical assistance, tell him all about the antihistamines (oral and topical) you used. The doctor will then be able decide the appropriate course of actions for the severity of your allergic reaction.

If you've been traveling (whether internationally or domestically), he may ask you if your travels have included staying in hotels or travelling.

A Few Prevention Measures

In order to stop the annoying pest from coming back, more is needed than a simple clean-up. It is well-known that pesticides are extremely effective at eliminating bed bugs. Moreover, because they thrive in temperate climates it is possible to help expose them to high temperatures.

You don't need to have only visited clean areas, as this fiendish species has also been seen in places where standards are high. It is all they need to find a safe, warm spot where they can hide and reproduce. The only thing they love is cluttered walls and rooms. You should clean out your room first before you take on a bug family.

Bed Bugs In Your Home

Your home is their destination

How much weight does a quarter-inch insect have? How much does an insect a quarter of an inch in length weigh? The reason it always finds its way to your home is because of your luggage, used furniture, bedding or other items. The bugs can be brought into the house by hopping on clothing or sewing seams. Bed bugs are often called so because they bite people as they sleep. But they can actually hide in any dark and soft place in your house.

The tiny bed bug can survive in nearly any environment that offers cover. They can use this to their advantage in reproduction, allowing them to lay eggs more easily and for longer. This patient bug will not die from starvation, even if it is left for an extended period of time without any blood. This means that you may find thousands of them in an unoccupied apartment, waiting for their meal at night.

There are bedbugs all around the globe. Bed bugs were thought to be more prevalent in developing countries, but today are an issue of concern for Northern Europe and America. These bugs can be found most often in areas such as motels and hotel rooms.

It is possible that you brought home bugs from furniture bought at garage sales or from books purchased in stores. Even brand new clothes can bring them into your home. Without you knowing, they can get into your purses, bags and shoes. But that is not all. It can also travel through walls and cracks to move between apartments and rooms within a complex.

In order to get rid of bugs, some neighbors use unapproved insecticides and bug bombs. They actually spread bugs by making them flea from one room to another.

For the night-time bug, cracks in ceilings and walls are the best hiding places. The long, dark yarns of carpets as well as the folds in curtains and seams on furniture are all suitable hiding spots. In mattress seams as well as headboards, bedsheet folds and springboards. Some of them are hiding behind tags and buttons. It is possible that the bugs are hiding in tiny screws and cracks found on footboards and bed frames.

Sometimes, you may not even notice that there are bugs in your home for a few weeks. When the bug infestation is more severe, it can be difficult to locate the source. If you can identify which pest family they belong to, it will be easier for you to track them down.

Chapter 19: Treatment And Prevention

You've probably tried to repel bedbugs more than a few times. Your house is clean, you've sprayed more insecticide and you even have flipped over your mattress more than the number of times you shop for groceries each month.

Just hold on.

While better housekeeping may increase your odds of cleaning bug stations in your home, or turning your mattress upside down will get rid of dust mites; these actions will by no means deter parasitic insects. Like cockroaches these parasites don't like filth. They require cozy, dark areas to reproduce during the day. However, at night they can sneak away and feed your blood.

Spraying pesticide indiscriminately is a waste of money and time. Sprays that aren't approved by EPA will simply spread the bugs around, leaving the homeowner with a much bigger problem. More rooms, more corners, more bugs!

No shortcut or easy solution exists to eliminate bug infestations. The pests are hard to spot during the daylight hours unless one looks really closely. Chances of success, however, are low unless one is determined. They will multiply from a handful to thousands in a matter of days if you don't take action. The bug must be tracked down and dealt with immediately.

The use of pesticides that are approved by the FDA and regularly cleaning your house will help you to live pest-free. You may not completely eliminate the pest, but consistent effort will ensure that you do.

The best way to get rid of bugs is by cleaning and vacuuming the infected area. Vacuum floor coverings, beds, curtain frames and bed frames. Pay particular attention to corners in dark areas that would be difficult to reach. To get maximum results, you should vacuum carpets at the corners and near walls. Dry steamers are also very effective in killing bed bugs, and the eggs they lay. This is because these insects cannot withstand high temperatures. Take care not to blow out the bugs.

You must use a firm brush to scrub mattress stitching, seams along with the mattresses themselves. This will remove all bugs and eggs. To kill bed bugs, wash your sheets and clothing frequently. Dry them on high heat. Box springs and mattress covers should be covered with vinyl for at least a few months. Use duct tape to seal tears. The bugs will be trapped in these areas and should die within several months. Also, it can be helpful to move beds from the wall in order for bugs that are coming through wall cracks and wall hangings not to find an easy way onto your mattress. The bedding should always be clean and stored in a closed closet. Seal any holes or cracks around pipes and wires.

While a good cleaning routine can help rid your home of pests, in the event of a large infestation, it's best to call a pest control company. You can either hire an experienced pest controller, or you can ask for customer reviews. When necessary, request eco-friendly alternatives.

It is important to clean and test the sample before you start. A professional pest controller can then suggest an eradication solution. Be sure to only use pesticides listed with bugs on their labels. Pesticides not approved by the FDA can have adverse effects for bugs and even humans. But you should know that spraying pesticides on their own will not be effective unless it is combined with intensive cleaning.

Preventive Measures

It is important to clean the house, even if there are no rashes across your arms or back. Bed bugs can be lurking under carpets or furniture, just waiting to emerge. They say that it is difficult to guard against bed bugs, but prevention is more effective than treatment. It's hard to argue with the idea that a spotless house is aesthetically pleasing, especially when it has gleaming floors and walls.

Don't bring used or worn-out mattresses, furniture and frames inside your home. It is best to have them thoroughly cleaned prior to bringing into the house to keep bugs out. You may have brought them in on your purse. This means that old things aren't the only thing carrying bugs. These bugs can quickly get into seams in mattresses or couches and they will be hidden for many days.

Remove the sheet from the mattress to check for specks on it. Sealing cracks and crevices will prevent insects from traveling from the neighbor's flat to your living room and kitchen. You should wash your hand immediately if you spot a bug or other insect on your clothing. Also, launder the clothes in high temperature. Sort your clothing into bags in case you traveled and use the maximum heat the fabric is able to withstand.

Investigate couches, pillows and mattress seams in your home. Find skin, eggs and rusty stains on any hidden surface. You shouldn't stop with that. If you see traces, clean them up. You can also open the screw holes in your furniture and check on windowsills.

Avoid missing tiny spots of bugs in areas that are dark or tight. You can use a spotlight or magnifying glasses. Many wall hangings, wooden picture frames and other objects can conceal bugs. Their camouflaged skin makes them hard to see. Also, loose wall wallpaper is a good place to hide insects. When your flooring is covered in carpet, pull back the edges to check underneath. If you pull up the edges of your carpet, you can see rust stains as well as feces.

You can eliminate the bugs by washing, scrubbing, or spraying them.

Bed Bugs on Pets

Can Pets be at Risk?

Bed bugs do not live on pets like fleas and ticks. Instead they are hidden in dark crevices. Bed bugs almost never choose pets over humans if given the chance. In order to determine the origin of the infestation in your home, you should assume the bugs were carried by your backpack on your return from work. This is a more reasonable assumption than assuming your cat or your dog was the culprit. Do not worry if you think your dog may be housing a bug colony.

Chapter 20: Treatments

Other Treatments

Since we've learned to be extra careful about this resilient, defensive insect (it is difficult to believe it can grow to a size of a quarter inch!) Rest assured, it's possible to eliminate bedbugs from your home. The guidelines include how to remove bugs from an infested residence, as well as how to disinfect the house. Most importantly, they also explain how to stop a future infestation. Stop giving your room adequate prevention care and the odds are that you will see a return.

Most bed bugs can be found in areas with high crowds. Bed bugs can spread from bags and clothing in a mall or movie theatre. If you're travelling, check your bags, luggage, bedding, and mattresses for bedbugs in the hotel.

In order to gain easy access into your bed, "Bed" insects can make themselves comfortable in the mattress seams. It is possible to cover mattresses and springs in zippered covers for a period of over one year. Bugs will be trapped and could die from starvation. The wallpaper that is peeling should be adhered down, while cracks within the wall can be plastered. This will prevent the bugs from using these hiding spots to reproduce during the daylight hours.

Do not place pet bedding near furniture or sleeping areas. You should regularly wash all the bedding, toys, clothes and pillows of your pet and then dry them on high temperatures (especially if your pet has just recently returned home from a holiday). Although bugs do not necessarily die after washing, they will be destroyed by temperatures reaching 120 degrees Fahrenheit when dried.

Avoid spreading bed bugs in other rooms by being extra cautious when transporting the bedding to your laundry. Separate the infected clothing from the other clothes and put it into plastic bags. When you finish washing the clothing that is infected with a fungus, seal it in a plastic container before transferring them to another room.

Keep your kids safe. You should clean your children's rooms and bedding regularly if you own pets. For a complete kill of bed bugs in soft toys (like stuffed bears), you can place them into the dryer for up to 30 minutes at high temperatures. Bed bugs also cannot tolerate temperatures that are lower than zero Fahrenheit (-18 Celsius). You can freeze plastic toys and other items such as jewelry, shoes or books for up to four full days. This will remove all signs of bed bug infestation. You can also spray toys with alcohol to eliminate bed bugs eggs. You can place the items you have cleaned into plastic bags while cleaning up the rest.

www.ingramcontent.com/pod-product-compliance
Lightning Source LLC
Chambersburg PA
CBHW071439080526
44587CB00014B/1919
* 9 7 8 1 7 7 7 5 9 7 6 8 9 *